# BR STANDARD STEAM LOCOMOTIVES

# BR
# STANDARD STEAM
# LOCOMOTIVES

**LOCOMOTIVES ILLUSTRATED**

## BRIAN STEPHENSON

LONDON

**IAN ALLAN LTD**

**First published 1983**
**Reprinted 1993**

ISBN 978-0-7110-1245-5

© **Ian Allan Ltd 1983**

**Published by Ian Allan Ltd, Shepperton, Surrey;**
**This edition produced by TAJ Books - 2007**
**Printed in China**

# Contents

**COVER: The last Pacific retained in service by British Railways, 'Britannia' Class 7 4-6-2 No 70013** *Oliver Cromwell* **departs from Carnforth with a William Deacon's Bank Club special returning to Stockport via Hellifield on 17 March 1968.** *Brian Stephenson*

**TITLE PAGE: Brand new Class '9F' 2-10-0 No 92014 brings a March-Temple Mills coal train up the Great Eastern line from Cambridge near Newport on 15 June 1954.**
*D. M. C. Hepburne-Scott, Rail Archive Stephenson*

**LEFT: 'Clan' Class Pacific No 72007** *Clan Mackintosh* **storms away from Beattock Station after stopping for a banker with the 09.25 Crewe-Perth train in June 1964.** *T. G. Hepburn, Rail Archive Stephenson*

# Preface

WHEN *Locomotives Illustrated* No 1 made its appearance in 1974, there was no telling that eight years later the series would still be going strong. Such is the continuing appeal of the steam locomotive that perhaps no one should be surprised at the success of this quarterly production. Those involved with the preparation of *Locomotives Illustrated* have staged the appearance of the locomotive classes so that all the aces — the popular classes — would not be played at once. However, more than one 'family' of classes has now been completed which explains the appearance of this book. Although it includes material from the five issues of *Locomotives Illustrated*, dealing with BR Standard locomotives, for reasons connected with

production it does not include every photograph featured in the separate magazines. Also, for reasons of space, it has not been practicable to reproduce the *Introductions* to each issue, but the full tabular matter is reproduced, updated and corrected as necessary.

The success of *Locomotives Illustrated* owes much to Brian Stephenson, the Picture Editor, who has put in so much work to ensure not only that each issue is comprehensive pictorially, but has prepared the tabular matter and looked out the best and most interesting photographs available. The publishers would like to take this opportunity to express their thanks.

*Michael Harris*
Series Editor

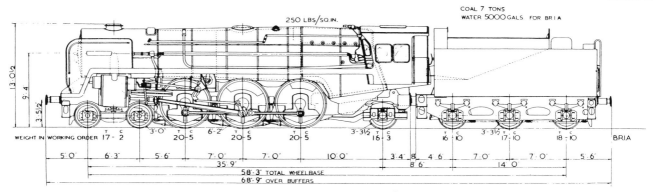

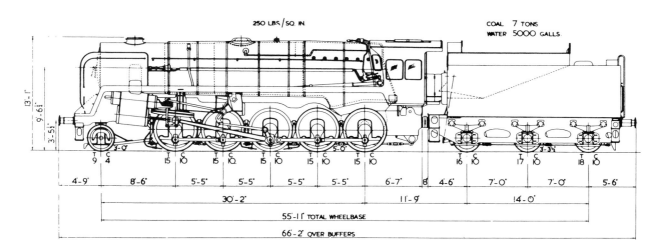

The first and last designs of the BR Standard range.

TOP: The 'Britannia' class introduced in 1951.

ABOVE: The '9F' class introduced in 1954.

# 1 The Standard Pacifics

Britannia Class 7 Nos 70000-54
Duke of Gloucester Class 8P No 71000
Clan Class 6 No 72000-9

BELOW: Destined to become the last Pacific in normal service on British Railways, 'Britannia' No 70013 *Oliver Cromwell* approaches Ipswich with the down 'Broadsman' from Liverpool Street on 7 July 1952. *John P. Wilson*

UPPER LEFT: The first 'Britannias' were allocated to the Great Eastern Line with a view to rejuvenating the service from London to East Anglia. They were the first Pacifics to work over the main lines from Liverpool Street. Here No 70001 *Lord Hurcomb* climbs Brentwood bank with the down 'Norfolkman', the 10.00 Liverpool Street-Norwich express on 24 March 1951. *E. D. Bruton*

LOWER LEFT: The down 'Broadsman' departs from Liverpool Street on 3 September 1951 hauled by 'Britannia' No 70013 *Oliver Cromwell*. *John P. Wilson*

BELOW: Another look at the 'Norfolkman', departing from Liverpool Street headed by 'Britannia' No 70002 *Geoffrey Chaucer* in 1951. *F. R. Hebron, Rail Archive Stephenson*

**UPPER LEFT:** No 70000 *Britannia* **itself heads the 14.05 Norwich-Liverpool Street relief at Mountnessing on 21 May 1951.** *R. E. Vincent*

**LOWER LEFT:** No 70030 *William Wordsworth* **leaves Cambridge with a Norwich-Liverpool Street express on 24 August 1957.** *T. G. Hepburn, Rail Archive Stephenson*

**TOP:** **The 09.45 Norwich-Liverpool Street express approaches Bentley hauled by No 70041** *Sir John Moore* **on 19 August 1960.** *G. R. Mortimer*

**ABOVE:** **No 70002** *Geoffrey Chaucer* **crosses Seven Arches Viaduct between Marks Tey and Colchester with the down 'Norfolkman' on 11 June 1951.** *C. W. Footer*

UPPER LEFT: Although initially allocated to the GE line, three 'Britannias' were soon transferred to the Southern Region. Here No 70009 *Alfred the Great* passes Clapham Junction with the down 'Bournemouth Belle' from Waterloo on 23 June 1951. No 70009 did not remain at Nine Elms for long and soon returned to the GE. *Brian Morrison*

LOWER LEFT: The other two 'Britannias' were allocated to Stewarts Lane for hauling the 'Golden Arrow' and other boat trains and stayed on the SR until 1958. No 70004 *William Shakespeare* passes Bickley with the down 'Golden Arrow' from Victoria in July 1955. *Brian Morrison*

ABOVE: Another look at No 70004 *William Shakespeare* as it departs from Victoria with the down 'Golden Arrow' on 6 July 1952. *John P. Wilson*

RIGHT: No 70014 *Iron Duke* leaves Dover with the up 'Golden Arrow' for London on 1 August 1954. The two Stewarts Lane 'Britannias' were always immaculately turned out. *W. A. Corkill*

**UPPER LEFT:** The next region to receive a large batch of 'Britannias' was the Western and they were all given old GWR names. Here No 70028 *Royal Star* approaches Craven Arms with a Swansea-Manchester train on 21 August 1954. *Donald Kelk*

**LOWER LEFT:** At 07.30 No 70021 *Morning Star* pulls out of St Erth with the overnight Paddington-Penzance sleeper on 14 April 1952. All the 'Britannias' between Nos 70000 and 70044, with the exception of Nos 70025-29, were coupled with the Type BR1 tender with a capacity of 4,250 gallons of water and seven tons of coal. *B. A. Butt*

**ABOVE:** The superbly named No 70018 *Flying Dutchman* rounds the curve from Reading West with the 13.30 Paddington-Plymouth express on 11 May 1955.
*D. M. C. Hepburne-Scott, Rail Archive Stephenson*

UPPER LEFT: No 70026 *Polar Star* glints in the evening sun as it hurries west with the 'Red Dragon' from Paddington to Cardiff meeting a '2251' class 0-6-0 labouring uphill towards Winterbourne with a long string of coal empties in Summer 1958.  *George Heiron*

LOWER LEFT: The up 'Red Dragon' heads out of Sonning Cutting east of Reading hauled by No 70029 *Shooting Star* on 19 April 1954. This was one of the five engines, Nos 70025-29, fitted with Type BR1A tenders having a larger water capacity of 5,000 gallons but the same seven ton coal space.  *T. E. Williams*

BELOW: No 70023 *Venus* accelerates out of Bath with the down 'Bristolian' from Paddington on 19 September 1952. Although originally scattered around the WR the 'Britannias' were eventually all shedded at Cardiff Canton.
*George Heiron*

ABOVE: 'Clan' Pacific No 72009 *Clan Stewart* has a tough assignment with the nine-coach 09.25 Crewe-Perth train seen climbing Beattock without banking assistance on 11 August 1964. The first five 'Clans' were allocated to Polmadie shed while the remainder went to Carlisle Kingmoor. *John S. Whiteley*

UPPER RIGHT: 'Clan' No 72001 *Clan Cameron* is brought to a stand at Greskine signalbox due to a derailment at Beattock summit while working a northbound stopping train. *Eric Treacy*

LOWER RIGHT: No 72006 *Clan Mackenzie* has the assistance of a banking engine as it climbs Beattock in the early morning with a northbound relief in August 1961. *W. J. Verden Anderson*

**UPPER LEFT:** The sole BR Standard class '8P' Pacific No 71000 *Duke of Gloucester* glints in the late afternoon sun as it climbs past Oxenholme with the down 16 vehicle 'Midday Scot' when new. *J. D. Mills*

**LOWER LEFT:** No 71000 *Duke of Gloucester* backs out of Euston after arrival with an express from Liverpool Lime Street on 24 April 1962. *Patrick Russell*

**BELOW:** The three-cylinder No 71000 was withdrawn from service in November 1962 after only eight and a half years' service. It then remained at Crewe for several years where it is seen on 16 April 1967 awaiting its call to the scrapyard. Its outside cylinders have been removed, one for display in the Science Museum, and the loco eventually went to Woodham's Barry scrapyard for breaking up. Like many engines sent to that now famous yard, it was rescued by a preservation society and today is undergoing restoration by the Duke of Gloucester Steam Locomotive Trust on the Great Central Railway at Loughborough. *P. Gerald*

**UPPER LEFT:** The final batch of 10 'Britannias' were coupled with large Type BR1D tenders which carried 4,725 gallons of water and nine tons of coal and gave the locos a much better appearance. The first five of this series were allocated to Holyhead where the earlier engines were found to have insufficient coal capacity on the run to Euston. Even so, No 70045 *Lord Rowallan* does not appear to have much coal left as it approaches Llandudno Junction with the down 'Irish Mail' overtaking a down ECS train hauled by a Stanier 'Jubilee' 4-6-0. *Kenneth Field*

**LOWER LEFT:** The final five were sent to Polmadie and given suitable names. Here No 70050 *Firth of Clyde* heads out of Carlisle with a Glasgow-Manchester and Liverpool express on 22 May 1956. *John P. Wilson*

**BELOW:** A stopping train for Carstairs departs from Edinburgh Princes Street station behind the final 'Britannia' No 70054 *Dornoch Firth*. *Eric Treacy*

**TOP:** After dieselisation of their duties on the GE lines the ER transferred several 'Britannias' to Immingham shed for workings to Kings Cross and other important turns. Here No 70035 *Rudyard Kipling* pounds up the 1 in 107 of Bleakhills bank near Mansfield with the 16.30 Class 'C' fish train from Grimsby to Whitland on 23 May 1962. *J. Cupit*

**ABOVE:** No 70040 *Clive of India* enters Boston with the 08.52 Cleethorpes-Kings Cross express in February 1961. *Les Perrin*

**UPPER RIGHT:** Still shedded at Immingham, No 70039 *Sir Christopher Wren* passes Sowerby Bridge with a Scunthorpe-Blackpool excursion on 8 September 1963. *John K. Morton*

**RIGHT:** Not long before its transfer to Immingham, No 70038 *Robin Hood* heads an up freight south of Barkston on the GN main line while returning to Norwich after overhaul, 15 July 1959.
*T. G. Hepburn, Rail Archive Stephenson*

**UPPER LEFT:** Now allocated to Willesden, No 70034 *Thomas Hardy* pulls away from East Leake with the 17.15 Nottingham Victoria-Marylebone semi-fast on 1 August 1963.
*T. G. Hepburn, Rail Archive Stephenson*

**LOWER LEFT:** No 70014 *Iron Duke* arrives at Nottingham Victoria with an afternoon semi-fast from Marylebone on 14 September 1962 when allocated to Annesley shed.
*T. G. Hepburn, Rail Archive Stephenson*

**BELOW:** Gradually all the 'Britannias' were allocated to the LMR and most ended their days at Carlisle Kingmoor working over the West Coast and Settle & Carlisle main lines. Here No 70009 *Alfred the Great*, still fitted with its SR lamp brackets, departs from Perth General with the 16.45 fish train to the south in April 1964.   *W. J. Verden Anderson*

**ABOVE:** 'Clan' Pacific No 72007, formerly *Clan Mackintosh*, heads the 16.37 Carlisle-Bradford stopping train through the Eden Valley near Armathwaite on 31 August 1965.  *S. C. Crook*

**LEFT:** Another view of No 72007 seen climbing Beattock near Harthope with the 09.25 Crewe-Perth train on 1 June 1963.  *Derek Cross*

**UPPER RIGHT:** An afternoon Liverpool-Glasgow express climbs past Greenholme on the ascent of Shap hauled by No 72003 *Clan Fraser* and banked by Fowler 2-6-4T No 42404 on 28 July 1960. The Polmadie 'clans' were all withdrawn at the end of 1962 in the great purge of express locos by the Scottish Region.
*Derek Cross*

**LOWER RIGHT:** No 72008 *Clan Macleod* departs from Perth with the 16.45 fish train in April 1964. The Kingmoor 'Clans' were gradually withdrawn as they fell due for repair and the last went in May 1966.
*W. J. Verden Anderson*

UPPER LEFT: 'Britannia' Pacific No 70050 Firth of Clyde passes Grayrigg with a down freight in April 1965. *Ivo Peters*

LOWER LEFT: No 70032 *Tennyson*, bereft of nameplates, climbs Shap near Shap Wells with a heavy northbound freight on 1 April 1967 banked by Fairburn 2-6-4T No 42252.
*T. G. Hepburn, Rail Archive Stephenson*

ABOVE: The 15.40 stopping train to Carlisle departs from Bradford Forster Square behind No 70051 (*Firth of Forth*) in April 1966.
*John S. Whiteley*

RIGHT: No 70001 (*Lord Hurcomb*) heads away from the camera as it leaves Bradford with the 15.40 to Carlisle in April 1966. *John S. Whiteley*

BELOW: With its name painted on its smoke deflectors, No 70038 *Robin Hood* gets a rare fling on express passenger work as it tops Shap summit with the Saturday 14.00 Glasgow-Manchester and Liverpool express on 22 July 1967. *Paul Claxton*

BELOW: Standard Class '4' 4-6-0 No 75063
runs light into Nottingham Midland on
12 October 1957.
*T. G. Hepburn, Rail Archive Stephenson*

**BELOW:** The first two Standard Class '5' 4-6-0s, Nos 73001 and 73000 head a special vacuum-fitted coal train during a controlled 40 mile/h test run near Harpenden on 26 October 1952.  *E. D. Bruton*

**BOTTOM:** No 73003 passes Mill Hill with a down semi-fast from St Pancras on 7 April 1953. The first five engines of the class were initially allocated to Derby and Leicester sheds where no doubt Derby Works personnel could keep a close watch on them.
*E. R. Wethersett, Real Photographs Company*

**UPPER RIGHT:** No 73002 crosses the River Trent as it leaves Nottingham with an Edinburgh-St Pancras express on 7 August 1954.  *John P. Wilson*

**LOWER RIGHT:** Nicely groomed No 73004 accelerates away from its stop at Kibworth with the 11.42 Northampton Castle-Leicester stopping train on 15 March 1952.  *A. F. Taylor*

LEFT: Class '5' No 73030 departs from Droylsden with a Leeds-Manchester stopping train. *Kenneth Field*

BELOW: An earlier view of No 73030 when fitted, in company with No 73031, with a Westinghouse brake pump for a series of air-braked freight train trails. It is seen heading out of Nottingham over the River Trent with the Sunday 16.15 express to St Pancras on 5 September 1954.
*T. G. Hepburn, Rail Archive Stephenson*

UPPER RIGHT: No 73044 climbs away from Bradford Exchange past Coal Shoots Cabin with an empty stock train. The first 50 Standard Class '5' 4-6-0s, Nos 73000-49, were fitted with the Type BR1 tender. *Kenneth Field*

LOWER RIGHT: In the early 1960s a number of Standard Class '5's were allocated to Woodford Halse. One of these, No 73010, has just left Barnston Tunnel with a Rugby-Nottingham Victoria stopping train.
*T. G. Hepburn, Rail Archive Stephenson*

UPPER LEFT: Brand new Standard Class '4' 4-6-0 No 75004 calls at Reading General with a Trowbridge-Paddington train on 3 September 1951. *John P. Wilson*

LOWER LEFT: Another almost new Class '4' 4-6-0, No 75059 waits to leave Nottingham Midland with the 14.30 stopping train to Chesterfield on 22 May 1957. *John P. Wilson*

TOP: No 75030 approaches Oxford with a cross country train from Bletchley. The Standard '4' 4-6-0s were fitted with the Type BR2 or BR2A tender up to No 75064. These carried 3,500 gallons of water and 6 tons of coal. *R. C. Riley*

ABOVE: The 15 Standard '4' 4-6-0s allocated to the Southern Region were given the Type BR1B tender with a capacity of 4,725 gallons and 7 tons of coal. Here No 75074 has an arduous duty as it crosses Riddlesdown Viaduct with a heavy evening Victoria-Tunbridge Wells commuter train in May 1959. *Derek Cross*

**TOP:** The first Standard Class '5' engines allocated to the Southern were Nos 73050-2 for use on the Somerset & Dorset line. They were joined later by others such as No 73054, in WR green livery, seen climbing Corfe Mullen bank with a Bank Holiday Bristol-Bournemouth excursion in June 1965. *M. K. Lewis*

**ABOVE:** Class '4' 4-6-0 No 75009 has just been attached to the northbound 'Pines Express' hauled by Class '9F' 2-10-0 No 92245 at Evercreech Junction for the climb over the Mendips on 18 August 1962. *G. A. Richardson*

**RIGHT:** A Bournemouth-Bristol stopping train arrives at Midford hauled by Class '4' No 75073. *Derek Cross*

**UPPER LEFT:** The first of the three Standard Class '5' 4-6-0s allocated new to the Somerset & Dorset line, No 73050, coasts down the Midford Valley with a Bristol-Bournemouth train in June 1959. These three, Nos 73050-2, were unique among their class in having the Type BR1G tender with a capacity of 5,000 gallons and 7 tons of coal.   *Derek Cross*

**LOWER LEFT:** Class '4' 4-6-0 No 75007 rolls into Radstock with a Templecombe-Bath train on 18 July 1963.   *Derek Cross*

**BELOW:** The last public excursion over the Somerset & Dorset line from Bristol to Bournemouth on 30 August 1965 climbs past the site of Corfe Mullen Halt behind Class '5' No 73068.   *M. K. Lewis*

**BOTTOM:** LMS Class '2P' 4-4-0 No 40634 pilots Standard Class '4' 4-6-0 No 75027 out of Devonshire Tunnel, Bath with a Bournemouth-Cleethorpes express in July 1959.   *Derek Cross*

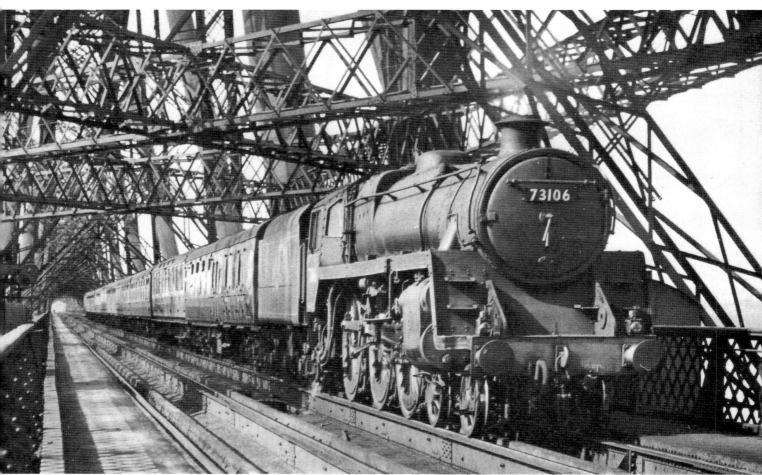

**UPPER LEFT: Class '5' 4-6-0 No 73006, complete with tablet exchanger for the Highland line, departs from Perth with the northbound 'Granite City' from Glasgow to Aberdeen.**
*T. G. Hepburn, Rail Archive Stephenson*

**LOWER LEFT: All the Class '5s' after No 73064 had flush-sided tenders — albeit of varying capacities. No 73106 seen here crossing the Forth Bridge with a Perth-Edinburgh express has a Type BR1B tender.**
*E. R. Wethersett, Real Photographs Company*

**ABOVE: No 73078 pilots a Thompson Class 'B1' 4-6-0 near Tulloch on the West Highland line with a Fort William-Glasgow train, 23 August 1960. The tender is of Type BR1C with a capacity of 4,725 gallons and 9 tons of coal, two tons more than carried in the Type BR1B tender on No 73106 opposite.** *S. C. Crook*

LEFT: The first of 30 Standard Class '5' 4-6-0s fitted with Caprotti valve gear, No 73125, heads the 14.50 Manchester Central-Derby train near Breadsall Crossing on 29 June 1956 while still in grey primer. *R. J. Buckley*

RIGHT: Caprotti Class '5' No 73140 makes a rare sight on the Southern as it passes East Croydon with a Leicester-Brighton excursion in July 1959. *Derek Cross*

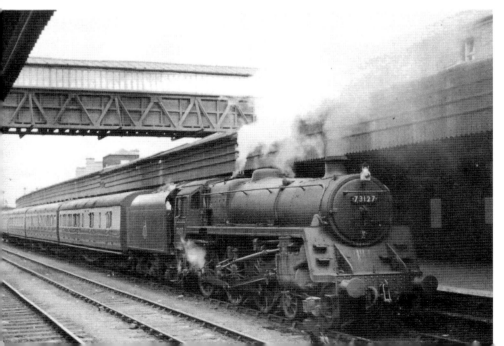

ABOVE: Caprotti '5' No 73142 pilots a 'Jubilee' 4-6-0 on a Manchester-St Pancras express seen passing Chinley North Junction on 24 August 1957. *Neville Fields*

LEFT: One of Shrewsbury's Caprotti engines, No 73127, waits to leave that City with the 10.10 train to Hereford on 10 June 1957. *M. Mensing*

RIGHT: A Leeds City-Sheffield Midland train arrives at Cudworth hauled by No 73144. Of the Caprotti engines ten each were originally allocated to the Western, London Midland and Scottish Regions. *Kenneth Field*

UPPER LEFT: Caprotti Class '5' No 73151 heads a northbound freight train in the Clyde Valley near Lamington during April 1961.   *Derek Cross*

LOWER LEFT: No 73151 is seen again as it departs from Gleneagles with the 16.14 Edinburgh Waverley-Perth train on 21 August 1964.   *John S. Whiteley*

TOP: Caprotti No 73150 climbs Kinbuck bank, north of Dunblane, with the 18.15 Glasgow Buchanan Street-Dundee train on 26 August 1965.   *Brian Stephenson*

ABOVE: The Caprotti Class '5' that ended its days at Ayr, No 73145, pilots Stanier Class '5' No 44999 through Ayr station with a goods from Stranraer on 5 July 1966.   *Derek Cross*

**UPPER LEFT:** An unidentified Standard Class '4' 4-6-0 heads back to Rhyl along the North Wales coast near Penmaenmawr with the Welsh Land Cruise circular tour train. *Kenneth Field*

**LOWER LEFT:** Standard Classes '4' and '5' at Leeds City with No 75047 setting empty stock back into the station and No 73065 waiting in the engine yard. *Kenneth Field*

**ABOVE:** Seven of the Standard Class '4' engines allocated to the Western and all those on the Southern were fitted with double chimneys from 1957 onwards. The first fitted was No 75029 seen climbing the 1 in 100 from Honeybourne to Chipping Camden with the 13.40 Hereford-Oxford train on 23 September 1957. *M. Mensing*

**RIGHT:** Another double chimney Class '4' No 75006, now London Midland Region stock due to regional boundary changes, waits to leave Chester General with the 17.55 train to Barmouth on 30 May 1964. *John S. Whiteley*

TOP: Standard Class '5' No 73088 waits to depart from Bournemouth Central with an express from Waterloo on 30 June 1958. *John P. Wilson*

ABOVE: Twenty of the Standard '5s' on the Southern were given the names from withdrawn 'King Arthur' 4-6-0s. No 73085 *Melisande* leaves the tunnel at the approach to Southampton Central with a Waterloo-Bournemouth express in June 1960. *Derek Cross*

UPPER RIGHT: No 73082 *Camelot* passes Vauxhall with the 11.30 Waterloo-Weymouth train on 27 September 1964. *Brian Stephenson*

LOWER RIGHT: The final ten Standard '5s' allocated to the SR, Nos 73110-9 were given the large Type BR1F tenders which carried 5,625 gallons and 7 tons of coal. Here No 73115 *King Pellinore* approaches Vauxhall and the 18.09 Waterloo-Basingstoke train on 2 September 1964. *Brian Stephenson*

ABOVE: Standard Class '4' and '5' 4-6-0s Nos 75075 and 73043 double-head the 16.46 Weymouth-Waterloo extra train out of Upwey South Tunnel on Easter Monday, 1967. No 75075 has acquired a Type BR1F tender from a withdrawn Class '5' while No 73043 is one of the several Class '5s' the SR obtained from other regions towards the end of steam. *John H. Bird*

LEFT: No 73086 *The Green Knight* whistles as it enters Fisherton Tunnel, Salisbury with an up West of England express for Waterloo on 22 August 1964. *Paul Riley*

UPPER RIGHT: A former NER Class '5' No 73168 approaches Clapham Junction with the 07.30 Basingstoke-Waterloo train on 2 July 1964. *Brian Stephenson*

LOWER RIGHT: No 73002 struggles unassisted up Medstead bank from Alton with the diverted 11.30 Waterloo-Weymouth train on 24 April 1966. *M. K. Lewis*

UPPER LEFT: The Standard Class '4' 4-6-0s were commonplace on both the routes to the Cambrian Coast from Ruabon and Shrewsbury. Here No 75027, supposedly in green livery, arrives at Bala Junction with the 14.35 Barmouth-Chester train on 23 July 1963. *Brian Stephenson*

LOWER LEFT: Another Welsh route over which both types of Standard 4-6-0 were used was the Central Wales line and two Class '5s', Nos 73026 and 73024 are changing places on the 12.25 Swansea Victoria-Shrewsbury train at Pontardulais, 19 November 1960. *H. Daniel*

TOP: The Standard '4s' were the last steam engines employed on the Cambrian line and No 75021 is seen topping the summit at Westbury while working the last down 'Cambrian Coast Express' forward from Shrewsbury to Aberystwyth on 4 March 1967. *Brian Stephenson*

ABOVE: Some of the Class '4' engines displaced from the Cambrian were sent north to act as banking engines at Tebay, the last steam engines to perform that duty. Here No 75026, with double chimney banks a northbound parcels train up Shap on 28 October 1967.
*T. G. Hepburn, Rail Archive Stephenson*

ABOVE: A few Standard '4s' survived into 1968 for working the Grassington Branch being based at Skipton and later, Carnforth. One of the last survivors, No 75019, leaves Swindon End with a ballast train for Skipton 31 May 1968.

BELOW: Nos 75019 and 75027 make one of their last runs with a Carnforth-Skipton special seen passing Hellifield on 28 July 1968. No 75027 survived to be preserved on the Bluebell Railway.
*Both: John S. Whiteley*

Class 4 Nos 76000-114
Class 3 Nos 77000-19
Class 2 Nos 78000-64

BELOW: Brand new Class '4' No 76089
approaches Beauchief with the 16.30 Sheffield
Midland-Manchester Central on 5 June 1957.
*K. S. Hudson*

ABOVE: A Gillingham-Salisbury school train leaves Semley in charge of Class '4' No 76008 on 8 June 1964. *Derek Cross*

LEFT: No 76014 gets moving out of Fratton with a Portsmouth-Cardiff train on 1 October 1961. *P. H. Wells*

UPPER RIGHT: No 76015 pilots Standard Class '5' 4-6-0 No 73050 on a Bristol-Bournemouth excursion train seen passing through Midsomer Norton station on the Somerset & Dorset Joint line, 5 June 1960. *Ivo Peters*

LOWER RIGHT: No 76025 arrives at Bournemouth West with a train from Salisbury as 'West Country' Pacific No 34106 *Lydford* waits to depart with the 11.05 to Waterloo on 11 April 1955.
*D. M. C. Hepburne-Scott, Rail Archive Stephenson*

LEFT: Class '4' No 76048 pauses at Kirkby Stephen East with a Penrith-Darlington train. Class '2' No 78014 is in the background.
*T. G. Hepburn, Rail Archive Stephenson*

BELOW: When new, ten of the Class '3' 2-6-0s were allocated to Darlington primarily for working over the Stainmore line. Here Nos 77004/10 join the 09.20 from Darlington to the 07.32 South Shields-Blackpool train at Tebay on 31 July 1954. The leading engine is fitted with a slip coupling and pulley rope for uncoupling after banking trains up to Stainmore Summit.
*J. E. Wilkinson*

UPPER RIGHT: Standard Class '4' No 76024 pilots one of its austere forebears, Ivatt Class '4' Mogul No 43129, out of Kirkby Stephen East on 6 August 1960 with a Newcastle-Blackpool train. *Derek Cross*

LOWER RIGHT: Class '4' 2-6-0s Nos 76022 (leading) and 76048 leave Tebay with a train of empty coke wagons for Durham on 16 June 1956. Nos 76000-44 were paired with the Type BR2 tender with flexible draught screens between engine and tender while all other engines in the class, except Nos 76053-69, had the Type BR2A which was coupled to engines with a modified cab which did away with the screens. Both tender types carried 3,500 gallons of water and 6 tons of coal *J. E. Wilkinson*

FAR LEFT ABOVE: Class '4' No 76024 heads out of Stockton with the Thornaby breakdown train.
*T. G. Hepburn, Rail Archive Stephenson*

FAR LEFT BELOW: A busy scene at Scarborough with Class '3' No 77004 standing in the Falsgrave platform after arrival from Darlington as Raven 'B16/1' 4-6-0 No 61470 heads out of the main station on a York train.
*T. G. Hepburn, Rail Archive Stephenson*

ABOVE: No 77001 departs from Knottingley with the 12.32 Wakefield Kirkgate-Goole in June 1957.   *P. Cookson*

LEFT: No 77014 climbs out of Haltwhistle with the 17.40 branch train to Alston on 4 July 1959.
*R. Leslie*

BELOW: No 77012 storms up the 1 in 39 to Ravenscar with a Darlington-Scarborough express on 2 September 1954.
*T. G. Hepburn, Rail Archive Stephenson*

TOP: The first ten Standard Class '2' Moguls went to the Western Region for service on the Cambrian lines. Green-liveried No 78006 heads a Welshpool-Machynlleth train near Carno in July 1962. *J. C. Beckett*

ABOVE: Now allocated to Gloucester, No 78004 waits to leave Hereford with the 16.30 train on its home city on 24 September 1964. *B. J. Ashworth*

UPPER RIGHT: No 78007 climbs out of Borth with the 16.15 Newtown-Aberystwyth on 19 July 1957. *S. Creer*

LOWER RIGHT: No 78001 passes through Chalford station with an inspection saloon on 9 June 1964. *Derek Cross*

**THIS PICTURE:** An interesting comparison is given in this view of Ivatt Class '2' 2-6-0 No 46404 piloting Standard Class '2' No 78028 at Huntingdon East on a Kettering-Cambridge train.
*T. G. Hepburn, Rail Archive Stephenson*

**BELOW:** No 78028, after modification to its cab roof to permit it to pass through the restricted Glenfield Tunnel which it is seen leaving with a goods train from Leicester West Bridge to Desford on 16 May 1964. *G. D. King*

**UPPER RIGHT:** The 15.40 Rochdale-Wigan passes Bury Gas Works Sidings on 9 June 1962 hauled by No 78043. *R. S. Greenwood*

**LOWER RIGHT:** No 78025 passes Long Eaton Junction with the 14.30 Nottingham Midland-Chesterfield on 9 May 1955. *John P. Wilson*

UPPER LEFT: Of the fifteen Class '4s' allocated to the Eastern Region, Nos 76030-34 went to Stratford and Nos 76035-44 to Neasden. Here brand-new No 76041 heads a down stopping train from Marylebone over the GW/GC Joint line near Denham in 1954.
*E. R. Wethersett, Ian Allan Library*

LOWER LEFT: Following the transfer of the Great Central line to the LMR, the Standard '4s' at Neasden were gradually displaced to other sheds in that Region. Here No 76038 puts on a brave show as it pilots Standard Class '4' 4-6-0 No 75010 on the up 'Cambrian Coast Express' between Llanbrynmair and Talerddig on 20 August 1966, shortly before it was withdrawn from Machynlleth shed. *C. F. Weston*

ABOVE: No 76089 passes under the Styal line at Didsbury with an eastbound express from Manchester Central. *Kenneth Field*

CENTRE RIGHT: By now allocated to Chester and minus its smokebox numberplate, No 76036 is seen between Rock Ferry and Bebington with the 08.55 Birkenhead-Paddington express in July 1966. *J. Taylor*

LOWER RIGHT: On the Great Central main line, No 76052 approaches Rushcliffe Halt with a Nottingham Victoria-Leicester Central stopping train.
*T. G. Hepburn, Rail Archive Stephenson*

**UPPER LEFT:** Newly transferred to Fort William shed, No 76001 approaches Lochailort with a Mallaig train on 12 August 1960. *D. M. C. Hepburne-Scott, Rail Archive Stephenson*

**LOWER LEFT:** Class '2' No 78048 leaves St Boswells with the 16.00 to Berwick upon Tweed on 31 August 1962. These engines had the Type BR3 tender which carried 3,000 gallons of water and four tons of coal. *T. G. Hepburn, Rail Archive Stephenson*

**BELOW:** North Blyth's Class '3' No 77011 leaves Woodburn with a pick-up goods on the former NBR line to Reedsmouth. *P. N. Townend*

**BOTTOM:** The 14.21 to St Boswells stands in Kelso station on 2 September 1963 with Class '2' No 78046 at the head of a single coach. *T. G. Hepburn, Rail Archive Stephenson*

TOP: Class '4' No 76105 crosses the River Fiddich as it leaves Craigellachie with the 09.00 Elgin-Aberdeen in September 1957. *W. J. Verden Anderson*

ABOVE: Another of Kittybrewster's Class '4' 2-6-0s, No 76106, heads a stopping train on the Great North of Scotland section in May 1958. *T. G. Hepburn, Rail Archive Stephenson*

UPPER RIGHT: Class '3' 2-6-0s No 77008/9 were allocated to Perth when new. No 77008 heads the 13.25 Blair Atholl-Perth stopping train near Dunkeld on 15 May 1954. *W. J. Verden Anderson*

LOWER RIGHT: The 14.55 Cragellachie-Boat of Garten heads away from Nethy Bridge behind Class '2' No 78054 in September 1957. *W. J. Verden Anderson*

BELOW: Class '3' No 77017 heads a lightweight Hurlford-New Cumnock pick-up freight near Polquhap summit on 3 June 1963.

RIGHT: No 77005 steams gently along the Clyde Valley main line near Wandel Mill with a northbound freight on 8 April 1961. *Both: Derek Cross*

ABOVE: No 76090 banks a northbound freight up Beattock near Harthope on 1 June 1963.

LEFT: Ayr's 'Pet', Class '4' No 76096, pulls out of Maybole on 5 March 1965 with an emergency Girvan-Ayr steam train. This was running in place of the usual dmu service through to Glasgow, the previous two days having had blizzard conditions. *Both: Derek Cross*

THIS PICTURE: Class '4' No 76055 pulls out of Oxted with a special for Tonbridge in May 1959. Nos 76053-69 were allocated to the SR and were given Type BR1B tenders with a capacity of 4,725 gallons of water and 7 tons of coal. *Derek Cross*

BELOW: No 76053 on the approach to Tonbridge as it leaves Somerhill Tunnel with a train from Brighton in March 1960. *Derek Cross*

UPPER RIGHT: On the Somerset & Dorset Joint line the single-line tablet is ready in the exchanger as No 76065 approaches Corfe Mullen with a northbound train on 14 September 1961. *D. M. C. Hepburne-Scott, Rail Archive Stephenson*

LOWER RIGHT: No 76063 on a freight for Southampton leaves the tunnel at the closed Winchester Chesil station on the former Didcot Newbury and Southampton line, 18 July 1962. *Brian Stephenson*

ABOVE: Class '4' No 76044 from Woodford Halse shed passes Clapham Junction with the 15.54 Waterloo-Basingstoke on 15 May 1964. It was en route to Eastleigh Works for repair at a time when Eastleigh was undertaking the repair of steam locomotives from the London Midland Region.
*Brian Stephenson*

## 4 The Standard Tanks
Class 4 Nos 80000-154
Class 3 Nos 82000-44
Class 2 Nos 84000-29

BELOW: Class '4' No 80130 departs from
Glasgow Central with a Hamilton train on
19 May 1956, *John P. Wilson*

UPPER LEFT: The first of the Class '4' tanks to be delivered was the batch numbered from 80010 built at Brighton; all went initially to Tunbridge Wells shed. Here brand new No 80016 heads the 15.35 Oxted-Brighton train near Newick on 24 September 1951. *S. C. Nash*

CENTRE LEFT: One of the later arrivals on the Central Section, No 80082 approaches Oxted on a Tunbridge Wells-London train in May 1959. *Derek Cross*

LOWER LEFT: The 11.55 Birmingham New Street-Eastbourne relief train passes through Kensington Olympia hauled by No 80011 on 25 July 1953. *S. C. Nash*

ABOVE: No 80013 is seen after arriving at Victoria with the 07.47 train from Tunbridge Wells West on June 1962. *Brian Stephenson*

UPPER LEFT: The final ten Class '2' 2-6-2Ts were allocated to the SR when new. Here the last member of the class, No 84029, leaves Sandling Junction with a Maidstone-Dover train in June 1960. *Derek Cross*

LOWER LEFT: The SR also received 16 of the Class '3' 2-6-2Ts, mainly for use in the West Country. No 82011 approaches Seaton Junction with an Axminster-Exeter train in September 1959. *Derek Cross*

TOP: A train of condemned wagons creaks its way into Horsted Keynes on the closed line from East Grinstead hauled by Class '4' No 80149 in April 1960. *Derek Cross*

ABOVE: No 80014 makes a rare appearance on the through train from Plymouth seen arriving at Brighton on 11 April 1964. *G. D. King*

**ABOVE: One of Bletchley's stud of Standard Class '4' tanks No 80039 approaches Watford Tunnel with a down local from Euston. These engines were also used on the Oxford-Cambridge cross country line.** *Brian Morrison*

**ABOVE:** A large batch of Standard '4' tanks went to the LT&SR line for the heavy Fenchurch Street suburban trains. No 80072 leaves Tilbury with an up train for Fenchurch Street.
*P. Ransome-Wallis*

**THIS PICTURE:** No 80070 tackles the 1 in 90 at the approach to Westcliff with a train from Fenchurch Street to Southend. *P. I. Paton*

TOP: Standard '4' tank No 80112 heads a Muirkirk-Carstairs train near Inches in September 1961. These tanks did a massive amount of work on the former Caledonian and Glasgow and South Western routes in the south-west of Scotland.

ABOVE: No 80021 approaches Ayr with an excursion train from Glasgow on 16 July 1963. Note that the cabside has a recess for a token exchange fitting.

UPPER RIGHT: An engine formerly allocated to the NER, No 80117, departs from Dumfries with a Stranraer train in April 1965.

LOWER RIGHT: No 80112 is seen again as it departs from Ayr with a parcels train for Kilmarnock in May 1964. This engine actually has a token exchanger fitted.  *All: Derek Cross*

UPPER LEFT: The first 20 Standard Class '2' 2-6-2Ts were widely scattered among LMR sheds. No 84003 was out on loan to Chester (West) shed when it was photographed at Upton with a Seacombe-Wrexham train. *Ian Allan Library*

CENTRE LEFT: No 84001 passes Crewe North Junction with a Crewe-Northwich push-and-push train. *P. Ransome-Wallis*

BELOW: The 16.50 Leicester-Burton-on-Trent train rounds Knighton North Curve with No 84006 piloting '2P' 4-4-0 No 40633 on 21 August 1954. *G. D. King*

UPPER RIGHT: No 84012 propels the 'Delph Donkey' push-and-pull train away from Measurements Halt on its journey down to Greenfield Junction and, eventually, Oldham in August 1954. *Kenneth Field*

LOWER RIGHT: A Bradford-Penistone train arrives at its destination hauled by No 84013 in June 1957. *Kenneth Field*

UPPER LEFT: Only five of the Standard Class '4' tanks were allocated to the NER when new. Freshly delivered No 80119 is seen leaving Grosmont with a Whitby-Stockton train.
*T. G. Hepburn, Rail Archive Stephenson*

LOWER LEFT: No 80117 pulls away from Hayburn Wyke with a Whitby-Scarborough train.
*T. G. Hepburn, Rail Archive Stephenson*

ABOVE: No 80118 passes an NER slotted-post signal as it approaches Grosmont with a Stockton-Whitby train.
*T. G. Hepburn, Rail Archive Stephenson*

RIGHT: All the NER Standard '4' tanks had been sent to Leeds Neville Hill shed when this picture was taken of No 80118 approaching Arthington round the curve from Bramhope Tunnel with a Leeds-Harrogate-Ripon express. They all ended their days on the Scottish Region.
*Kenneth Field*

LEFT: A pair of Standard Class '3' tanks, Nos 82006 and 82034, head the northbound 'Devonian' near Torre en route for Newton Abbot on 26 May 1956. *R. J. Buckley*

RIGHT: No 82039 leaves Bridgend by the former Vale of Glamorgan line with the 13.50 train to Barry on 4 July 1955. *S. Rickard*

BELOW: The Machynlleth-Barmouth pick-up freight leaves Towyn hauled by green liveried No 82003 on 6 September 1962. *P. H. Wells*

LEFT: No 82037 brings a GWR design engineers' inspection saloon through Radstock on the Somerset and Dorset line on 18 July 1963. *Derek Cross*

RIGHT: Another green Class '3' 2-6-2T, No 82004, approaches Bewdley with the 13.45 Shrewsbury-Hartlebury train on 20 June 1959. The Tenbury branch can be seen going off on the left to cross the River Severn. *M. Mensing*

ABOVE: Western Region No 82030 leans to the curve as it accelerates over the summit of the climb from Savernake Low Level with the midday train from Andover to Swindon Town on 1 November 1959. *D. Fereday Glen*

LEFT: Exmouth Junction's No 82010 arrives at Sidmouth with the branch train from Sidmouth Junction on 3 September 1955. *G. D. King*

RIGHT: Made redundant on the LT&SR line by electrification, Class '4' 2-6-4T No 80135 finds a new home on the Cambrian line. It is heading an Aberystwyth-Oswestry train near Commins Coch on 4 June 1964. *Derek Cross*

**ABOVE:** Another migrant from the LT&SR line, No 80096, approaches Shepton Mallet on the Somerset and Dorset line with an afternoon Bath Green Park-Templecombe train on 1 January 196● *Brian Stephenson*

**UPPER RIGHT:** On the last day of service on the Somerset and Dorset line, 5 March 1966, No 80● leaves Chilcompton Tunnel with the 16.25 Bath Green Park-Templecombe train. *Brian Stephenso●*

**LOWER RIGHT:** Later the same day, No 80043 returns from Templecombe as pilot to No 80041 ● the last train from Bournemouth to Bath Green Park. They are taking water at Evercreech Junction prior to tackling the climb over the Mendips for the last time. No 80043 worked an RCTS special ov● the line the next day and was then withdrawn for scrap in company with her two surviving sisters at Templecombe. *Paul Riley*

**UPPER LEFT:** During the last week of steam working on the Swanage branch, Class '4' 2-6-4T No 80134 takes the branch at Worgret Junction with the 13.25 from Wareham on 31 August 1966. *John H. Bird*

**CENTRE LEFT:** As a result of Regional boundary changes, the London Midland Region took over some Standard Class '3' 2-6-2Ts which then found their way to new pastures. Here Patricroft-based No 82003 waits to leave Manchester Central with the LCGB 'Cotton Spinner' rail tour of 16 April 1966. *Ian G. Holt*

**BELOW:** The last Class '3' 2-6-2Ts were to be found on the SR at Nine Elms for working empty stock trains in and out of Waterloo. No 82019 passes Vauxhall with ecs from Clapham Junction to Waterloo in April 1967. *Brian Stephenson*

BELOW: Class '9F' 2-10-0 No 92071 nears the
end of its journey from Woodford Halse with a
train of coal empties as it takes the loop down to
the GN Leen Valley Line from the GC main line
at Bulwell Common 27 June 1957.
*T. G. Hepburn, Rail Archive Stephenson*

# 5 The Class 9F 2-10-0s
Nos 92000-250

RIGHT: A Leeds-London express freight heads south from Redhill Tunnel (Trent) behind '9F' No 92164 on 10 May 1958. The field on the right is now occupied by the massive Ratcliffe-on-Soar power station.
*T. G. Hepburn, Rail Archive Stephenson*

BELOW: '9F' No 92123 passes through Kettering with a down freight on the Nottingham line on 17 May 1957. *P. H. Wells*

LEFT: A Toton-Brent coal train approaches Mill Hill behind one of the 10 Crosti-boilered Class '9F' 2-10-0s, No 92026, on 20 April 1956. *A. R. Carpenter*

RIGHT: Another Crosti '9F', No 92021 enters the loop at Brentingby Junction (south of Melton Mowbray) with a southbound coal train from Toton on 2 August 1955. When running the exhaust from these engines came from the chimney close to the cab on the fireman's side. The orthodox chimney was only used for lighting-up. *T. G. Hepburn, Rail Archive Stephenson*

UPPER LEFT: One of the hardest duties undertaken by the '9Fs' was working iron ore trains from Tyne Dock to Consett. These trains were normally composed of nine bogie hopper wagons and a brakevan; the total weight averaged 787 tons to be hauled up gradients as steep as 1 in 35 in places. Here No 92097, banked by sister No 92066, storm the climb near Oxhill with an iron ore train for Consett on 19 April 1964. *A. R. Thompson*

LOWER LEFT: No 92064 coasts downgrade towards Pelaw South Junction with a train of iron ore empties bound for Tyne Dock on 29 August 1965. The 10 '9Fs' allocated to Tyne Dock for these workings were fitted with two air pumps midway along the running plate for operating the doors on the hopper wagons. *Brian Stephenson*

ABOVE: Another iron ore train for Consett eases past Pelaw South Junction behind No 92060 before taking on a banking engine for the climb to Consett in August 1966. *Verdun Wake*

LEFT: A coal train for Consett passes Pelaw South Junction on snowy 2 March 1965, hauled by '9F' No 92062. *John Hunt*

BELOW: A Doncaster '9F', No 92177, heads north with an oil tank train on the NER York-Darlington 'race track' near Benningborough, 6 August 1961. *G. W. Morrison*

UPPER RIGHT: No 92188 heads an up freight past Greenwood towards New Barnet in July 1959. *Derek Cross*

LOWER RIGHT: A southbound express freight rounds the curve at High Dyke into Stoke Tunnel behind No 92141 on 2 August 1958. The '9Fs' were fitted with a variety of tenders according to which region they were allocated. The ER engines illustrated here have Type BR1F with a capacity of 5,625 gallons of water and 7 tons of coal. The NER engines and the Crosti engines had Type BR1B carrying 4,725 gallons and 7 tons of coal. *G. W. Morrison*

FAR LEFT ABOVE: From 1957 Annesley GC shed was allocated nearly 30 '9Fs' under ER auspices and they became legendary for their handling of the Annesley-Woodford 'runners', as the coal trains were known. No 92094 approaches Rushcliffe Halt, south of Nottingham, with an up freight in 1963 after the line had been transferred to LMR control.

FAR LEFT BELOW: A northbound express freight approaches Bulwell Common behind No 92076.

ABOVE: Nos 92093 and 92069 double head a rather short up Class '8' freight south of East Leake on 31 July 1963.

LEFT: Nos 92031 and 92095 hurry south through Ruddington with a brakevan on 20 April 1964. Withdrawal of freight services on the GC main line brought the exploits of the '9Fs' on the Great Central to an end.
*ALL: T. G. Hepburn, Rail Archive Stephenson*

**LEFT:** The 10.48 Eastbourne-Sheffield Victoria train climbs towards Saunderton behind No 92132 from Annesley shed on 15 August 1964.   *Gerald T. Robinson*

**ABOVE:** No 92207, less than a month old, departs from Newport with the 09.20 Swansea-Brockenhurst train on 27 June 1959.   *J. Hodge*

UPPER LEFT: No 92221 enters the loop at Winchester Chesil on the Didcot, Newbury & Southampton Line with a train of empty oil tank wagons for the Esso refinery at Fawley on 18 July 1962. *Brian Stephenson*

LOWER LEFT: Another Esso train from Fawley heads north, loaded towards Southcote Junction, Reading hauled by No 92234 from Tyseley shed on 16 May 1964. *Brian Stephenson*

ABOVE: No 92205 heads a down pigeon special away from Southampton Central in 31 May 1963. This was one of five '9Fs' allocated at one time to the SR at Eastleigh ostensibly for working the oil trains from Fawley. These engines which came from the WR were unique in the class for their five-position dual type lamp brackets. *R. A. Panting*

RIGHT: Another odd duty for an Eastleigh '9F' is the 10.57 Salisbury-Portsmouth parcels train seen here at Southampton Central behind No 92231 which was working as far as Southampton Terminus on 1 February 1961. *J. C. Haydon*

**BELOW:** Bath Green Park shed managed to procure the use of No 92220 *Evening Star* to haul the last 'Pines Express' for Bournemouth seen roaring past Midford on 8 September 1962. *C. P. Boocock*

**BOTTOM:** No 92204 climbs away from Bath on 29 March 1960 during a trial run over the Somerset & Dorset line prior to the introduction of the class to the line for the summer service. *Ivo Peters*

**UPPER RIGHT:** No 92206 leaves Midsomer Norton with the 09.55 Bath Green Park-Bournemouth train on 19 August 1960. *Derek Cross*

**BOTTOM RIGHT:** A few of the earlier single chimney '9Fs' were later fitted with double chimneys at Swindon. One of them, No 92006 leaves Chilcompton Tunnel with the 07.45 Bradford-Bournemouth train on 12 August 1961. *M. J. Fox*

ABOVE: No 92009 heads a northbound van train at Carlisle Upperby as a southbound train of forgings gets under way behind a 'Britannia' Pacific in May 1965.   *W. J. Verden Anderson*

UPPER RIGHT: Former Crosti '9F' No 92024 pulls away from Beattock Station banked in the rear by a 2-6-4T with a Shap Quarry-Glasgow limestone train in 1964.
*T. G. Hepburn Rail Archive Stephenson*

LOWER RIGHT: No 92024 is seen again in 1964 breasting Beattock summit with a down mineral train as the 2-6-4T banker drops behind.   *T. G. Hepburn, Rail Archive Stephenson*

LEFT: No 92012, banked in the rear by a 2-6-4T, passes Greskine signalbox on the climb to Beattock summit with a Shap Quarry-Glasgow limestone train on 27 July 1964.
*John S. Whiteley*

BELOW: A southbound empty stock train threads the Lune Gorge south of Tebay behind No 92249, returning after the Glasgow Fair Holiday on 1 August 1964.
*W. J. Verden Anderson*

RIGHT: No 92208 climbs away towards Shap summit on 31 March 1967, with a southbound freight train. It has acquired a Type BR1C tender in place of its original Type BR1G.
*Brian Stephenson*

# BR STANDARD CLASSES
## SUMMARY OF NUMBERS, NAMES, DATES AND ALLOCATIONS

## BRITANNIA Class 7 4-6-2

| BR No | Name | Date Built | Withdrawn | First Shed | Allocation 7/62 | Final Shed | Notes |
|---|---|---|---|---|---|---|---|
| 70000 | Britannia | 1/51 | 5/66 | Stratford | Norwich | Newton Heath | 1 |
| 70001 | Lord Hurcomb | 2/51 | 9/66 | Stratford | March | Carlisle Kingmoor | |
| 70002 | Geoffrey Chaucer | 3/51 | 1/67 | Stratford | March | Carlisle Kingmoor | |
| 70003 | John Bunyan | 3/51 | 3/67 | Stratford | March | Carlisle Kingmoor | |
| 70004 | William Shakespeare | 3/51 | 12/67 | Stratford | Willesden | Carlisle Kingmoor | |
| 70005 | John Milton | 4/51 | 7/67 | Stratford | March | Carlisle Kingmoor | |
| 70006 | Robert Burns | 4/51 | 5/67 | Stratford | March | Carlisle Kingmoor | |
| 70007 | Coeur-de-Lion | 4/51 | 6/65 | Stratford | March | Carlisle Kingmoor | |
| 70008 | Black Prince | 4/51 | 1/67 | Norwich | March | Carlisle Kingmoor | |
| 70009 | Alfred the Great | 5/51 | 1/67 | Norwich | March | Carlisle Kingmoor | |
| 70010 | Owen Glendower | 5/51 | 9/67 | Norwich | March | Carlisle Kingmoor | |
| 70011 | Hotspur | 5/51 | 12/67 | Norwich | March | Carlisle Kingmoor | |
| 70012 | John of Gaunt | 5/51 | 12/67 | Norwich | March | Carlisle Kingmoor | |
| 70013 | Oliver Cromwell | 5/51 | 8/68 | Norwich | March | Carnforth | 2 |
| 70014 | Iron Duke | 6/51 | 12/67 | Norwich | Annesley | Carlisle Kingmoor | |
| 70015 | Apollo | 6/51 | 8/67 | Camden | Annesley | Carlisle Kingmoor | |
| 70016 | Ariel | 6/51 | 8/67 | Holbeck | Longsight | Carlisle Kingmoor | |
| 70017 | Arrow | 6/51 | 9/66 | Old Oak Common | Aston | Carlisle Kingmoor | |
| 70018 | Flying Dutchman | 6/51 | 12/66 | Old Oak Common | Longsight | Carlisle Kingmoor | |
| 70019 | Lightning | 6/51 | 3/66 | Newton Abbot | Longsight | Carlisle Upperby | |
| 70020 | Mercury | 7/51 | 1/67 | Old Oak Common | Longsight | Carlisle Kingmoor | |
| 70021 | Morning Star | 8/51 | 12/67 | Laira | Willesden | Carlisle Kingmoor | |
| 70022 | Tornado | 8/51 | 12/67 | Laira | Longsight | Carlisle Kingmoor | |
| 70023 | Venus | 8/51 | 12/67 | Old Oak Common | Longsight | Carlisle Kingmoor | |
| 70024 | Vulcan | 10/51 | 12/67 | Laira | Aston | Carlisle Kingmoor | |
| 70025 | Western Star | 9/52 | 12/67 | Cardiff Canton | Aston | Carlisle Kingmoor | |
| 70026 | Polar Star | 10/52 | 1/67 | Cardiff Canton | Aston | Stockport Edgeley | |
| 70027 | Rising Star | 10/52 | 6/67 | Cardiff Canton | Aston | Carlisle Kingmoor | |
| 70028 | Royal Star | 10/52 | 9/67 | Cardiff Canton | Longsight | Carlisle Kingmoor | |
| 70029 | Shooting Star | 11/52 | 10/67 | Cardiff Canton | Aston | Carlisle Kingmoor | |
| 70030 | William Wordsworth | 11/52 | 6/66 | Holyhead | March | Carlisle Upperby | |
| 70031 | Byron | 11/52 | 11/67 | Holyhead | Aston | Carlisle Kingmoor | |
| 70032 | Tennyson | 12/52 | 9/67 | Holyhead | Willesden | Carlisle Kingmoor | |
| 70033 | Charles Dickens | 12/52 | 7/67 | Holyhead | Willesden | Carlisle Kingmoor | |
| 70034 | Thomas Hardy | 12/52 | 5/67 | Longsight | March | Carlisle Kingmoor | |
| 70035 | Rudyard Kipling | 12/52 | 12/67 | Norwich | Immingham | Carlisle Kingmoor | |
| 70036 | Boadicea | 12/52 | 10/66 | Stratford | Immingham | Carlisle Kingmoor | |
| 70037 | Hereward the Wake | 12/52 | 11/66 | Stratford | Immingham | Carlisle Kingmoor | |
| 70038 | Robin Hood | 1/53 | 8/67 | Stratford | Immingham | Carlisle Kingmoor | |
| 70039 | Sir Christopher Wren | 2/53 | 9/67 | Norwich | Immingham | Carlisle Kingmoor | |
| 70040 | Clive of India | 3/53 | 4/67 | Norwich | Immingham | Carlisle Kingmoor | |
| 70041 | Sir John Moore | 3/53 | 4/67 | Stratford | Immingham | Carlisle Kingmoor | |
| 70042 | Lord Roberts | 4/53 | 5/67 | Stratford | Willesden | Carlisle Kingmoor | |
| 70043 | Lord Kitchener | 6/53 | 8/65 | Longsight | Aston | Crewe South | |
| 70044 | Earl Haig | 6/53 | 10/66 | Longsight | Holbeck | Stockport Edgeley | |
| 70045 | Lord Rowallen | 6/54 | 12/67 | Holyhead | Aston | Carlisle Kingmoor | |
| 70046 | Anzac | 7/54 | 7/67 | Holyhead | Aston | Carlisle Kingmoor | |
| 70047 | | 7/54 | 7/67 | Holyhead | Aston | Carlisle Kingmoor | |
| 70048 | The Territorial Army 1908-1958 | 8/54 | 5/67 | Holyhead | Annesley | Carlisle Kingmoor | |
| 70049 | Solway Firth | 8/54 | 12/67 | Holyhead | Annesley | Carlisle Kingmoor | |
| 70050 | Firth of Clyde | 8/54 | 8/66 | Polmadie | Corkerhill | Carlisle Kingmoor | |
| 70051 | Firth of Forth | 8/54 | 12/67 | Polmadie | Corkerill | Carlisle Kingmoor | |
| 70052 | Firth of Tay | 8/54 | 3/67 | Polmadie | Corkerhill | Carlisle Kingmoor | |
| 70053 | Moray Firth | 9/54 | 4/67 | Polmadie | Holbeck | Carlisle Kingmoor | |
| 70054 | Dornoch Firth | 9/54 | 11/66 | Polmadie | Holbeck | Carlisle Kingmoor | |

## DUKE OF GLOUCESTER Class 8P 4-6-2

| BR No | Name | Date Built | Withdrawn | First Shed | Allocation 7/62 | Final Shed | Notes |
|---|---|---|---|---|---|---|---|
| 71000 | Duke of Gloucester | 5/54 | 11/62 | Crewe North | Crewe North | Crewe North | 3 |

## CLAN Class 6 4-6-2

| BR No | Name | Date Built | Withdrawn | First Shed | Allocation 7/62 | Final Shed | Notes |
|---|---|---|---|---|---|---|---|
| 72000 | Clan Buchanan | 12/51 | 12/62 | Polmadie | Polmadie | Polmadie | |
| 72001 | Clan Cameron | 12/51 | 12/62 | Polmadie | Polamdie | Polmadie | |
| 72002 | Clan Campbell | 1/52 | 12/62 | Polmadie | Polmadie | Polmadie | |
| 72003 | Clan Fraser | 1/52 | 12/62 | Polmadie | Polmadie | Polmadie | |
| 72004 | Clan Macdonald | 2/52 | 12/62 | Polmadie | Pomadie | Polmadie | |
| 72005 | Clan Macgregor | 2/52 | 4/65 | Carlisle Kingmoor | Carlisle Kingmoor | Carlisle Kingmoor | |
| 72006 | Clan Mackenzie | 2/52 | 5/66 | Carlisle Kingmoor | Carlisle Kingmoor | Carlisle Kingmoor | |
| 72007 | Clan Mackintosh | 2/52 | 12/65 | Carlisle Kingmoor | Carlisle Kingmoor | Carlisle Kingmoor | |
| 72008 | Clan Macleod | 2/52 | 4/66 | Carlisle Kingmoor | Carlisle Kingmoor | Carlisle Kingmoor | |
| 72009 | Clan Stewart | 3/52 | 8/65 | Carlisle Kingmoor | Carlisle Kingmoor | Carlisle Kingmoor | |

*Building Details: 70000-24 built at Crewe, order No E479. 70025-44 built at Crewe, order No E483. 70045-54 built at Crewe, order No E486. 71000 built at Crewe, order No E486. 72000-09 built at Crewe, order No E480.*

NOTES: 1) Preserved by the Britannia Locomotive Society, locations vary.

2) Last BR Standard Pacific in service, owned by National Railway Museum, located at Bressingham Steam Museum.

3) Rescued from Woodhams, Barry scrapyard in 1973 by Duke of Gloucester Steam Locomotive Trust. Restored at Loughborough, Great Central Railway, and now located at Didcot Railway Centre.

# Class 5 4-6-0

| BR No | Date Built | Date Withdrawn | First Shed | Final Shed | Notes |
|---|---|---|---|---|---|
| 73000 | 4/51 | 3/68 | Derby | Patricroft | |
| 73001 | 5/51 | 12/65 | Derby | Bath Green Park | |
| 73002 | 5/51 | 3/67 | Derby | Weymouth | |
| 73003 | 6/51 | 12/65 | Leicester | Oxford | |
| 73004 | 6/51 | 10/67 | Leicester | Bolton | |
| 73005 | 6/51 | 6/66 | Perth | Corkerhill | |
| 73006 | 6/51 | 3/67 | Perth | Patricroft | |
| 73007 | 7/51 | 3/66 | Perth | Stirling | |
| 73008 | 7/51 | 9/65 | Perth | Ferryhill | |
| 73009 | 7/51 | 7/66 | Perth | Corkerhill | |
| 73010 | 8/51 | 6/68 | Holbeck | Patricroft | |
| 73011 | 8/51 | 11/67 | Holbeck | Patricroft | |
| 73012 | 8/51 | 11/64 | Holbeck | Bristol Barrow Road | |
| 73013 | 8/51 | 5/66 | Sheffield Millhouses | Bolton | |
| 73014 | 9/51 | 7/67 | Sheffield Millhouses | Bolton | |
| 73015 | 9/51 | 8/65 | Sheffield Millhouses | Bath Green Park | |
| 73016 | 9/51 | 12/66 | Sheffield Grimesthorpe | Weymouth | |
| 73017 | 9/51 | 10/64 | Nottingham | Weymouth | |
| 73018 | 10/51 | 7/67 | Nottingham | Guildford | |
| 73019 | 10/51 | 1/67 | Nottingham | Bolton | |
| 73020 | 10/51 | 7/67 | Chester | Guildford | |
| 73021 | 10/51 | 8/65 | Chester | Oxford | |
| 73022 | 10/51 | 4/67 | Chester | Nine Elms | |
| 73023 | 11/51 | 8/65 | Patricroft | Oxford | |
| 73024 | 11/51 | 11/64 | Patricroft | Oxford | |
| 73025 | 11/51 | 10/67 | Blackpool | Patricroft | |
| 73026 | 11/51 | 4/67 | Blackpool | Bolton | |
| 73027 | 12/51 | 2/64 | Blackpool | Swindon | |
| 73028 | 12/51 | 12/66 | Blackpool | Bolton | |
| 73029 | 1/52 | 7/67 | Blackpool | Nine Elms | |
| 73030 | 6/53 | 8/65 | Derby | Oxford | |
| 73031 | 7/53 | 9/65 | Derby | Oxford | |
| 73032 | 7/53 | 8/65 | Carlisle Kingmoor | Croes Newydd | |
| 73033 | 8/53 | 1/68 | Polmadie | Patricroft | |
| 73034 | 8/53 | 3/68 | Carlisle Kingmoor | Patricroft | |
| 73035 | 8/53 | 1/68 | Polmadie | Patricroft | |
| 73036 | 9/53 | 9/65 | Carlisle Kingmoor | Shrewsbury | |
| 73037 | 9/53 | 7/67 | Shrewsbury | Nine Elms | |
| 73038 | 9/53 | 10/65 | Chester | Shrewsbury | |
| 73039 | 9/53 | 9/67 | St Philip's Marsh | Patricroft | |
| 73040 | 10/53 | 5/68 | Chester | Patricroft | |
| 73041 | 10/53 | 6/65 | Chester | Guildford | |
| 73042 | 10/53 | 8/65 | Chester | Weymouth | |
| 73043 | 10/53 | 7/67 | Patricroft | Nine Elms | |
| 73044 | 11/53 | 3/65 | Patricroft | Oxford | |
| 73045 | 11/53 | 8/67 | Holbeck | Patricroft | |
| 73046 | 11/53 | 9/64 | Leicester | Nine Elms | |
| 73047 | 12/53 | 12/64 | Sheffield Millhouses | Shrewsbury | |
| 73048 | 12/53 | 10/67 | Sheffield Milhouses | Bolton | |
| 73049 | 12/53 | 3/65 | Leicester | Oxford | |
| 73050 | 6/54 | 6/68 | Bath Green Park | Patricroft | 1 |
| 73051 | 6/54 | 8/65 | Bath Green Park | Bath Green Park | |
| 73052 | 6/54 | 12/64 | Bath Green Park | Bath Green Park | |
| 73053 | 6/54 | 3/68 | Holbeck | Patricroft | |
| 73054 | 6/54 | 8/65 | Holbeck | Bath Green Park | |
| 73055 | 6/54 | 5/66 | Polmadie | Polmadie | |
| 73056 | 7/54 | 6/65 | Polmadie | Ferryhill | |
| 73057 | 7/54 | 3/66 | Polmadie | Corkerhill | |
| 73058 | 7/54 | 11/64 | Polmadie | Ferryhill | |
| 73059 | 8/54 | 5/67 | Polmadie | Polmadie | |
| 73060 | 8/54 | 5/67 | Polmadie | Polmadie | |
| 73061 | 9/54 | 12/64 | Polmadie | Polmadie | |
| 73062 | 9/54 | 6/65 | Polmadie | Polmadie | |
| 73063 | 9/54 | 6/66 | Polmadie | Polmadie | |
| 73064 | 10/54 | 5/67 | Polmadie | Polmadie | |
| 73065 | 10/54 | 7/67 | Sheffield Millhouses | Nine Elms | |
| 73066 | 10/54 | 4/67 | Holbeck | Bolton | |
| 73067 | 10/54 | 3/68 | Nottingham | Patricroft | |
| 73068 | 10/54 | 12/65 | Derby | Bath Green Park | |
| 73069 | 11/54 | 8/68 | Derby | Carnforth | |
| 73070 | 11/54 | 4/67 | Chester | Bolton | |
| 73071 | 11/54 | 9/67 | Chester | Patricroft | |
| 73072 | 12/54 | 10/66 | Chester | Polmadie | |
| 73073 | 12/54 | 11/67 | Patricroft | Patricroft | |
| 73074 | 12/54 | 9/64 | Patricroft | Nine Elms | |
| 73075 | 4/55 | 12/65 | Polmadie | Polmadie | |
| 73076 | 4/55 | 7/64 | Polmadie | Polmadie | |
| 73077 | 5/55 | 12/64 | Eastfield | Corkerhill | |
| 73078 | 5/55 | 7/66 | Eastfield | Kipps | |
| 73079 | 5/55 | 5/67 | Eastfield | Polmadie | |
| 73080 | 6/55 | 12/66 | Stewarts Lane | Weymouth | |
| 73081 | 6/55 | 7/66 | Stewarts Lane | Guildford | |
| 73082 | 6/55 | 6/66 | Stewarts Lane | Guildford | 2 |
| 73083 | 7/55 | 9/66 | Stewarts Lane | Weymouth | |
| 73084 | 7/55 | 12/65 | Stewarts Lane | Eastleigh | |
| 73085 | 8/55 | 7/67 | Stewarts Lane | Nine Elms | |
| 73086 | 8/55 | 10/66 | Stewarts Lane | Nine Elms | |
| 73087 | 8/55 | 10/66 | Stewarts Lane | Guildford | |
| 73088 | 9/55 | 10/66 | Stewarts Lane | Guildford | |
| 73089 | 9/55 | 9/66 | Stewarts Lane | Guildford | |
| 73090 | 10/55 | 10/65 | Patricroft | Shrewsbury | |
| 73091 | 10/55 | 5/65 | Patricroft | Gloucester | |
| 73092 | 10/55 | 7/67 | Patricroft | Guildford | |
| 73093 | 11/55 | 7/67 | Patricroft | Guildford | |
| 73094 | 11/55 | 5/67 | Patricroft | Patricroft | 3 |
| 73095 | 11/55 | 8/66 | Patricroft | Agecroft | |
| 73096 | 11/55 | 11/67 | Patricroft | Patricroft | |
| 73097 | 12/55 | 5/67 | Patricroft | Patricroft | |
| 73098 | 12/55 | 3/66 | Patricroft | Polmadie | |
| 73099 | 12/55 | 10/66 | Patricroft | Polmadie | |
| 73100 | 8/55 | 1/67 | Corkerhill | Corkerhill | |
| 73101 | 8/55 | 8/66 | Corkerhill | Corkerhill | |
| 73102 | 9/55 | 12/66 | Corkerhill | Corkerhill | |
| 73103 | 9/55 | 10/65 | Corkerhill | Corkerhill | |
| 73104 | 9/55 | 10/65 | Corkerhill | Corkerhill | |
| 73105 | 12/55 | 9/66 | Eastfield | Corkerhill | |
| 73106 | 12/55 | 6/66 | Eastfield | Corkerhill | |
| 73107 | 12/55 | 9/66 | Eastfield | Motherwell | |
| 73108 | 12/55 | 12/66 | Eastfield | Carstairs | |
| 73109 | 1/56 | 10/64 | Eastfield | Eastfield | |
| 73110 | 10/55 | 1/67 | Nine Elms | Guildford | |
| 73111 | 10/55 | 9/65 | Nine Elms | Eastleigh | |
| 73112 | 10/55 | 6/65 | Nine Elms | Nine Elms | |
| 73113 | 10/55 | 1/67 | Nine Elms | Weymouth | |
| 73114 | 11/55 | 6/66 | Nine Elms | Weymouth | |
| 73115 | 11/55 | 3/67 | Nine Elms | Guildford | |
| 73116 | 11/55 | 11/64 | Nine Elms | Eastleigh | |
| 73117 | 11/55 | 3/67 | Nine Elms | Guildford | |
| 73118 | 12/55 | 7/67 | Nine Elms | Guildford | |
| 73119 | 12/55 | 3/67 | Nine Elms | Eastleigh | |
| 73120 | 1/56 | 12/66 | Perth | Corkerhill | |
| 73121 | 1/56 | 2/66 | Corkerhill | Corkerhill | |
| 73122 | 1/56 | 9/65 | Corkerhill | Corkerhill | |
| 73123 | 2/56 | 5/65 | Corkerhill | Corkerhill | |
| 73124 | 2/56 | 12/65 | Corkerhill | Corkerhill | |
| 73125 | 7/56 | 6/68 | Shrewsbury | Patricroft | 4 |
| 73126 | 7/56 | 4/68 | Shrewsbury | Patricroft | 4 |
| 73127 | 8/56 | 11/67 | Shrewsbury | Patricroft | 4 |
| 73128 | 8/56 | 5/68 | Shrewsbury | Patricroft | 4 |
| 73129 | 8/56 | 11/67 | Shrewsbury | Patricroft | 4, 5 |
| 73130 | 9/56 | 1/67 | Shrewsbury | Patricroft | 4 |
| 73131 | 9/56 | 1/68 | Shrewsbury | Patricroft | 4 |
| 73132 | 10/56 | 3/68 | Shrewsbury | Patricroft | 4 |
| 73133 | 10/56 | 6/68 | Shrewsbury | Patricroft | 4 |
| 73134 | 10/56 | 6/68 | Shrewsbury | Patricroft | 4 |
| 73135 | 10/56 | 3/68 | Holyhead | Patricroft | 4 |
| 73136 | 11/56 | 3/68 | Holyhead | Patricroft | 4 |
| 73137 | 11/56 | 6/67 | Holyhead | Patricroft | 4 |
| 73138 | 11/56 | 4/68 | Holyhead | Patricroft | 4 |
| 73139 | 11/56 | 5/67 | Holyhead | Patricroft | 4 |
| 73140 | 12/56 | 10/67 | Leicester | Patricroft | 4 |
| 73141 | 12/56 | 7/67 | Leicester | Patricroft | 4 |
| 73142 | 12/56 | 4/68 | Leicester | Patricroft | 4 |
| 73143 | 12/56 | 6/68 | Leicester | Patricroft | 4 |
| 73144 | 12/56 | 8/67 | Leicester | Patricroft | 4 |
| 73145 | 1/57 | 9/66 | St Rollox | Ayr | 4 |
| 73146 | 2/57 | 5/67 | St Rollox | Polmadie | 4 |
| 73147 | 2/57 | 8/65 | St Rollox | St Rollox | 4 |
| 73148 | 3/57 | 9/65 | St Rollox | St Rollox | 4 |
| 73149 | 3/57 | 12/66 | St Rollox | Stirling | 4 |
| 73150 | 4/57 | 12/66 | St Rollox | Stirling | 4 |
| 73151 | 4/57 | 8/66 | St Rollox | St Rollox | 4 |
| 73152 | 5/57 | 12/65 | St Rollox | St Rollox | 4 |
| 73153 | 5/57 | 12/66 | St Rollox | Stirling | 4 |
| 73154 | 6/57 | 12/66 | St Rollox | Motherwell | 4 |
| 73155 | 12/56 | 7/67 | Neasden | Guildford | |
| 73156 | 12/56 | 11/67 | Neasden | Bolton | |
| 73157 | 12/56 | 5/68 | Neasden | Patricroft | |
| 73158 | 12/56 | 10/67 | Neasden | Patricroft | |
| 73159 | 1/57 | 9/67 | Neasden | Patricroft | |
| 73160 | 1/57 | 11/67 | Blaydon | Patricroft | |
| 73161 | 2/57 | 12/64 | Blaydon | Exmouth Junction | |
| 73162 | 2/57 | 5/65 | York | Oxford | |
| 73163 | 2/57 | 11/65 | York | Patricroft | |
| 73164 | 3/57 | 12/64 | York | Oxford | |

| BR No | Date Built | Date Withdrawn | First Shed | Final Shed | Notes |
|---|---|---|---|---|---|
| 73165 | 3/57 | 10/65 | York | Patricroft | |
| 73166 | 3/57 | 12/65 | York | Oxford | |
| 73167 | 4/57 | 8/65 | York | Shrewsbury | |
| 73168 | 4/57 | 12/65 | York | Eastleigh | |
| 73169 | 4/57 | 10/66 | York | Eastleigh | |
| 73170 | 5/57 | 6/66 | York | Eastleigh | |
| 73171 | 5/57 | 10/66 | York | Eastleigh | |

## NAMED LOCOMOTIVES

73080 Merlin
73081 Excalibur
73082 Camelot
73083 Pendragon
73084 Tintagel
73085 Melisande
73086 The Green Knight
73087 Linette
73088 Joyous Gard
73089 Maid of Astolat
73110 The Red Knight
73111 King Uther
73112 Morgan le Fay
73113 Lyonnesse
73114 Etarre
73115 King Pellinore
73116 Iseult
73117 Vivien
73118 King Leodegrance
73119 Elaine

## BUILDING DETAILS

73000-29 Built at Derby, order No 5122
73030-49 Built at Derby, order No 6230
73050-59 Built at Derby, order No 6735
73060-64 Built at Derby, order No 8035
73065-74 Built at Derby, order No 8025
73075-89 Built at Derby, order No 8241
73090-99 Built at Derby, order No 8845
73100-104 Built at Doncaster, engine order No 402
73105-109 Built at Doncaster, engine order No 404
73110-119 Built at Doncaster, engine order No 403
73120-124 Built at Doncaster, engine order No 404 (continued)
73125-154 Built at Derby, order No 9247
73155-164 Built at Doncaster, engine order No 406
73165-171 Built at Doncaster, engine order No 407

# Class 4 4-6-0

| BR No | Date Built | Date Withdrawn | First Shed | Final Shed | Notes |
|---|---|---|---|---|---|
| 75000 | 5/51 | 12/65 | Swindon | Worcester | |
| 75001 | 8/51 | 12/64 | Shrewsbury | Yeovil | |
| 75002 | 8/51 | 8/67 | Shrewsbury | Stoke | |
| 75003 | 8/51 | 10/65 | Shrewsbury | Worcester | 6 |
| 75004 | 8/51 | 3/67 | Bristol Bath Road | Shrewsbury | |
| 75005 | 9/51 | 11/65 | Shrewsbury | Worcester | 6 |
| 75006 | 9/51 | 8/67 | Swindon | Stoke | 6 |
| 75007 | 9/51 | 4/65 | Shrewsbury | Yeovil | |
| 75008 | 10/51 | 12/65 | Shrewsbury | Worcester | 6 |
| 75009 | 10/51 | 8/68 | Shrewsbury | Carnforth | |
| 75010 | 11/51 | 10/67 | Patricroft | Carnforth | |
| 75011 | 11/51 | 11/66 | Patricroft | Skipton | |
| 75012 | 11/51 | 1/67 | Patricroft | Shrewsbury | |
| 75013 | 11/51 | 8/67 | Patricroft | Stoke | |
| 75014 | 12/51 | 12/66 | Patricroft | Shrewsbury | 11 |

| BR No | Date Built | Date Withdrawn | First Shed | Final Shed | Notes |
|---|---|---|---|---|---|
| 75015 | 12/51 | 12/67 | Southport | Carnforth | |
| 75016 | 1/52 | 7/67 | Southport | Colwick (stationary boiler) | |
| 75017 | 1/52 | 1/67 | Southport | Skipton | |
| 75018 | 3/52 | 6/67 | Southport | Stoke | |
| 75019 | 3/52 | 8/68 | Southport | Carnforth | |
| 75020 | 11/53 | 8/68 | Oswestry | Carnforth | 6 |
| 75021 | 11/53 | 2/68 | Cardiff Canton | Carnforth | |
| 75022 | 12/53 | 12/65 | Cardiff Canton | Worcester | |
| 75023 | 12/53 | 1/66 | Oswestry | Stoke | |
| 75024 | 12/53 | 11/67 | Oswestry | Tebay | |
| 75025 | 4/54 | 12/65 | Laira | Worcester | |
| 75026 | 5/54 | 12/67 | Laira | Tebay | 6 |
| 75027 | 5/54 | 8/68 | Laira | Carnforth | 7 |
| 75028 | 5/54 | 12/65 | Laira | Machynlleth | |
| 75029 | 5/54 | 8/67 | Laira | Stoke | 6, 8 |
| 75030 | 6/53 | 12/67 | Bletchley | Tebay | |
| 75031 | 6/53 | 2/66 | Bletchley | Stoke | |
| 75032 | 6/53 | 2/68 | Bletchley | Carnforth | |
| 75033 | 7/53 | 12/67 | Bletchley | Carnforth | |
| 75034 | 7/53 | 2/68 | Bletchley | Carnforth | |
| 75035 | 8/53 | 7/67 | Bletchley | Tebay | |
| 75036 | 8/53 | 6/66 | Bletchley | Stoke | |
| 75037 | 8/53 | 12/67 | Bletchley | Tebay | |
| 75038 | 8/53 | 12/65 | Bletchley | Shrewsbury | |
| 75039 | 8/53 | 9/67 | Bletchley | Tebay | |
| 75040 | 8/53 | 10/67 | Bedford | Carnforth | |
| 75041 | 9/53 | 1/68 | Bedford | Carnforth | |
| 75042 | 9/53 | 11/67 | Bedford | Carnforth | |
| 75043 | 9/53 | 12/67 | Bedford | Carnforth | |
| 75044 | 9/53 | 3/66 | Bedford | Skipton | |
| 75045 | 9/53 | 4/66 | Accrington | Nuneaton | |
| 75046 | 10/53 | 8/67 | Accrington | Stoke | |
| 75047 | 10/53 | 8/67 | Accrington | Stoke | |
| 75048 | 10/53 | 8/68 | Accrington | Carnforth | |
| 75049 | 10/53 | 10/66 | Accrington | Bank Hall | |
| 75050 | 11/56 | 11/66 | Llandudno Junction | Stoke | |
| 75051 | 11/56 | 10/66 | Chester | Skipton | |
| 75052 | 12/56 | 8/67 | Bletchley | Stoke | |
| 75053 | 1/57 | 9/66 | Chester | Shrewsbury | |
| 75054 | 1/57 | 8/66 | Chester | Stoke | |
| 75055 | 1/57 | 5/67 | Bedford | Stoke | |
| 75056 | 3/57 | 6/66 | Nottingham | Stoke | |
| 75057 | 3/57 | 2/66 | Leicester | Skipton | |
| 75058 | 4/57 | 12/67 | Leicester | Carnforth | |
| 75059 | 4/57 | 7/67 | Leicester | Carnforth | |
| 75060 | 5/57 | 4/67 | Leicester | Croes Newydd | |
| 75061 | 5/57 | 2/67 | Leicester | Aintree | |
| 75062 | 5/57 | 2/68 | Nottingham | Carnforth | |
| 75063 | 6/57 | 5/66 | Nottingham | Shrewsbury | |
| 75064 | 6/57 | 5/67 | Nottingham | Aintree | |
| 75065 | 8/55 | 9/66 | Dover | Eastleigh | 6 |
| 75066 | 9/55 | 1/66 | Dover | Eastleigh | 6 |
| 75067 | 9/55 | 10/64 | Dover | Eastleigh | 6 |
| 75068 | 9/55 | 7/67 | Dover | Eastleigh | 6 |
| 75069 | 9/55 | 9/66 | Dover | Eastleigh | 6, 9 |
| 75070 | 10/55 | 9/66 | Exmouth Junction | Eastleigh | 6 |
| 75071 | 10/55 | 8/67 | Exmouth Junction | Stoke | 6 |
| 75072 | 11/55 | 12/65 | Exmouth Junction | Templecombe | 6 |
| 75073 | 11/55 | 12/65 | Exmouth Junction | Templecombe | 6 |
| 75074 | 11/55 | 7/67 | Exmouth Junction | Eastleigh | 6 |
| 75075 | 11/55 | 7/67 | Exmouth Junction | Eastleigh | 6 |
| 75076 | 12/55 | 7/67 | Exmouth Junction | Eastleigh | 6 |
| 75077 | 12/55 | 7/67 | Exmouth Junction | Eastleigh | 6 |
| 75078 | 1/56 | 7/66 | Exmouth Junction | Eastleigh | 6, 10 |
| 75079 | 1/56 | 11/66 | Exmouth Junction | Eastleigh | 6, 12 |

## BUILDING DETAILS

75000-09 Built at Swindon, lot No 390
75010-19 Built at Swindon, lot No 391
75020-29 Built at Swindon, lot No 400
75030-49 Built at Swindon, lot No 401
75050-64 Built at Swindon, lot No 408
75065-79 Built at Swindon, lot No 409

## NOTES for both classes

1) Withdrawn by the WR in 4/64 and reinstated by LMR in the same month. Now preserved on the Nene Valley Railway and named *City of Peterborough*.
2) Rescued from Woodhams, Barry scrapyard by the 73082 *Camelot* Locomotive Society at Sheffield Park on the Bluebell Railway.
3) Withdrawn by the WR and reinstated by the LMR in 5/64
4) Fitted with British Caprotti valve gear.
5) Rescued from Woodhams, Barry scrapyard by the Midland Railway Trust, Butterley and undergoing restoration.
6) Fitted from 1957 onwards with double blastpipe and chimney.
7) Preserved at Sheffield Park on the Bluebell Railway.
8) Preserved by the artist David Shepherd on the East Somerset Railway, Cranmore.
9) Rescued from Woodhams, Barry scrapyard and preserved on the Severn Valley Railway, Bridgnorth.
10) Rescued from Woodhams, Barry scrapyard and preserved on the Keighley & Worth Valley Railway, Haworth.
11) Rescued from Woodhams, Barry scrapyard and undergoing restoration on the North Yorkshire Moors Railway, Grosmont.
12) Rescued from Woodhams, Barry Scrapyard and undergoing restoration on the Plym Valley Railway, Plymouth.

# Class 4 2-6-0

| BR No | Date Built | Date Withdrawn | First Shed | Final Shed | Notes |
|-------|-----------|----------------|------------|------------|-------|
| 76000 | 12/52 | 5/67 | Motherwell | Motherwell | |
| 76001 | 12/52 | 8/66 | Motherwell | Ayr | |
| 76002 | 12/52 | 1/67 | Motherwell | Motherwell | |
| 76003 | 12/52 | 3/66 | Motherwell | Motherwell | |
| 76004 | 12/52 | 10/66 | Motherwell | Polmadie | |
| 76005 | 12/52 | 7/67 | Eastleigh | Bournemouth | |
| 76006 | 1/53 | 7/67 | Eastleigh | Bournemouth | |
| 76007 | 1/53 | 7/67 | Eastleigh | Bournemouth | |
| 76008 | 2/53 | 5/67 | Eastleigh | Bournemouth | |
| 76009 | 2/53 | 7/67 | Eastleigh | Bournemouth | |
| 76010 | 3/53 | 9/66 | Eastleigh | Bournemouth | |
| 76011 | 3/53 | 7/67 | Eastleigh | Bournemouth | |
| 76012 | 4/53 | 9/66 | Eastleigh | Guildford | |
| 76013 | 4/53 | 9/66 | Eastleigh | Bournemouth | |
| 76014 | 5/53 | 9/66 | Eastleigh | Bournemouth | |
| 76015 | 5/53 | 10/65 | Eastleigh | Bournemouth | |
| 76016 | 5/53 | 10/66 | Eastleigh | Guildford | |
| 76017 | 6/53 | 7/65 | Eastleigh | Salisbury | 1 |
| 76018 | 6/53 | 10/66 | Eastleigh | Guildford | |
| 76019 | 7/53 | 2/66 | Eastleigh | Eastleigh | |
| 76020 | 12/52 | 4/66 | Darlington | Chester | |
| 76021 | 12/52 | 10/66 | York | Hurlford | |
| 76022 | 12/52 | 8/66 | Dairycoates | Oxley | |
| 76023 | 12/52 | 10/65 | Sunderland | Stoke | |
| 76024 | 1/53 | 12/66 | Gateshead | Hurlford | |
| 76025 | 10/53 | 10/65 | Eastleigh | Bournemouth | |
| 76026 | 10/53 | 7/67 | Eastleigh | Bournemouth | |
| 76027 | 10/53 | 10/65 | Eastleigh | Bournemouth | |
| 76028 | 10/53 | 5/64 | Eastleigh | Eastleigh | |
| 76029 | 11/53 | 10/64 | Eastleigh | Eastleigh | |
| 76030 | 11/53 | 4/65 | Stratford | Eastleigh | |
| 76031 | 11/53 | 7/67 | Stratford | Guildford | |
| 76032 | 12/53 | 8/64 | Stratford | Guildford | |
| 76033 | 12/53 | 2/67 | Stratford | Guildford | |
| 76034 | 12/53 | 9/64 | Stratford | Guildford | |
| 76035 | 5/54 | 5/66 | Neasden | Chester | |
| 76036 | 6/54 | 1/67 | Neasden | Chester | |
| 76037 | 6/54 | 6/67 | Neasden | Croes Newydd | |
| 76038 | 7/54 | 9/66 | Neasden | Machynlleth | |
| 76039 | 7/54 | 6/67 | Neasden | Croes Newydd | |
| 76040 | 7/54 | 4/67 | Neasden | Croes Newydd | |
| 76041 | 7/54 | 4/67 | Neasden | Chester | |
| 76042 | 8/54 | 6/66 | Neasden | Oxley | |
| 76043 | 8/54 | 9/66 | Neasden | Machynlleth | |
| 76044 | 8/54 | 10/66 | Neasden | Chester | |
| 76045 | 3/55 | 1/66 | Gateshead | Carstairs | |
| 76046 | 3/55 | 5/67 | Gateshead | Corkerhill | |
| 76047 | 3/55 | 12/66 | Gateshead | Chester | |
| 76048 | 3/55 | 2/67 | Gateshead | Croes Newydd | |
| 76049 | 4/55 | 1/66 | Gateshead | Bathgate | |
| 76050 | 8/56 | 9/65 | Darlington | Hawick | |
| 76051 | 8/56 | 4/67 | York | Sutton Oak | |
| 76052 | 9/56 | 12/66 | York | Chester | |
| 76053 | 4/55 | 1/67 | Redhill | Guildford | |
| 76054 | 4/55 | 10/64 | Redhill | Guildford | |
| 76055 | 4/55 | 10/65 | Redhill | Salisbury | |
| 76056 | 5/55 | 11/65 | Redhill | Bournemouth | |
| 76057 | 5/55 | 10/66 | Redhill | Bournemouth | |
| 76058 | 6/55 | 3/67 | Redhill | Guildford | |
| 76059 | 6/55 | 9/66 | Redhill | Guildford | |
| 76060 | 7/55 | 12/65 | Redhill | Eastleigh | |
| 76061 | 7/55 | 1/67 | Redhill | Eastleigh | |
| 76062 | 7/55 | 10/65 | Redhill | Eastleigh | |
| 76063 | 7/56 | 4/67 | Eastleigh | Eastleigh | |
| 76064 | 7/56 | 7/67 | Eastleigh | Eastleigh | |
| 76065 | 7/56 | 10/65 | Eastleigh | Eastleigh | |
| 76066 | 7/56 | 7/67 | Eastleigh | Eastleigh | |
| 76067 | 8/56 | 7/67 | Eastleigh | Bournemouth | |
| 76068 | 8/56 | 10/65 | Eastleigh | Eastleigh | |
| 76069 | 8/56 | 6/67 | Eastleigh | Guildford | |
| 76070 | 9/56 | 8/66 | Motherwell | Polmadie | |
| 76071 | 10/56 | 1/66 | Motherwell | Polmadie | |
| 76072 | 10/56 | 10/64 | Dumfries | Dumfries | |
| 76073 | 10/56 | 6/66 | Dumfries | Ayr | |
| 76074 | 11/56 | 10/66 | Eastfield | Ayr | |
| 76075 | 12/56 | 10/67 | Sutton Oak | Springs Branch | |
| 76076 | 12/56 | 11/66 | Sutton Oak | Sutton Oak | |
| 76077 | 12/56 | 12/67 | Sutton Oak | Springs Branch | 3 |
| 76078 | 12/56 | 12/66 | Sutton Oak | Sutton Oak | |
| 76079 | 2/57 | 12/67 | Sutton Oak | Springs Branch | 2 |
| 76080 | 2/57 | 12/67 | Lower Darwen | Springs Branch | |
| 76081 | 2/57 | 7/67 | Lower Darwen | Springs Branch | |
| 76082 | 3/57 | 10/66 | Lower Darwen | Sutton Oak | |
| 76083 | 3/57 | 10/66 | Lower Darwen | Sutton Oak | |
| 76084 | 4/57 | 12/67 | Lower Darwen | Springs Branch | 8 |
| 76085 | 4/57 | 7/66 | Leicester (Mid) | Annesley | |
| 76086 | 5/57 | 9/66 | Leicester (Mid) | Croes Newydd | |
| 76087 | 5/57 | 1/67 | Trafford Park | Oxley | |
| 76088 | 5/57 | 6/67 | Trafford Park | Chester | |
| 76089 | 6/57 | 9/66 | Trafford Park | Annesley | |
| 76090 | 6/57 | 12/66 | Corkerhill | Beattock | |
| 76091 | 6/57 | 12/66 | Corkerhill | Hurlford | |
| 76092 | 6/57 | 8/66 | Corkerhill | Hurlford | |
| 76093 | 7/57 | 2/67 | Corkerhill | Corkerhill | |
| 76094 | 8/57 | 5/67 | Corkerhill | Beattock | |
| 76095 | 8/57 | 3/67 | Corkerhill | Chester | |
| 76096 | 9/57 | 12/66 | Corkerhill | Ayr | |
| 76097 | 9/57 | 7/64 | Corkerhill | Ayr | |
| 76098 | 10/57 | 5/67 | Corkerhill | Beattock | |
| 76099 | 11/57 | 8/66 | Corkerhill | Annesley | |
| 76100 | 5/57 | 8/66 | Dawsholm | Ayr | |
| 76101 | 6/57 | 12/66 | Dawsholm | Ayr | |
| 76102 | 6/57 | 12/66 | Parkhead | Hurlford | |
| 76103 | 6/57 | 7/66 | Parkhead | Ayr | |
| 76104 | 7/57 | 5/67 | Kittybrewster | Polmadie | |
| 76105 | 7/57 | 1/66 | Kittybrewster | Polmadie | |
| 76106 | 7/57 | 9/65 | Kittybrewster | Willesden | |
| 76107 | 8/57 | 10/65 | Kittybrewster | Bathgate | |
| 76108 | 8/57 | 7/66 | Kittybrewster | Hurlford | |
| 76109 | 8/57 | 9/66 | Thornton | Dunfermline | |
| 76110 | 8/57 | 12/66 | Thornton | Dunfermline | |
| 76111 | 8/57 | 1/66 | Thornton | Bathgate | |
| 76112 | 9/57 | 10/65 | Dumfries | Stranraer | |
| 76113 | 10/57 | 12/66 | St Rollox | Carstairs | |
| 76114 | 10/57 | 12/66 | St Rollox | Beattock | |

**Building details**

76000-76019 Horwich
76020-76024 Doncaster, Engine Order No 395
76025-76034 Doncaster, Engine Order No 396
76035-76044 Doncaster, Engine Order No 397
76045-76049 Doncaster, Engine Order No 401
76050-76052 Doncaster, Engine Order No 399
76053-76062 Doncaster, Engine Order No 400
76063-76069 Doncaster, Engine Order No 399 (Continued)
76070-76074 Doncaster, Engine Order No 405
76075-76099 Horwich, Lot No 249
76100-76109 Doncaster, Engine Order No 408
76110-76114 Doncaster, Engine Order No 409

# Class 3 2-6-0

| BR No | Date Built | Date Withdrawn | First Shed | Final Shed | Notes | BR No | Date Built | Date Withdrawn | First Shed | Final Shed | Notes |
|---|---|---|---|---|---|---|---|---|---|---|---|
| 77000 | 2/54 | 12/66 | Darlington | Stourton | | 77012 | 6/54 | 6/67 | Darlington | York | |
| 77001 | 2/54 | 1/66 | Darlington | Goole | | 77013 | 7/54 | 3/66 | Darlington | Stourton | |
| 77002 | 3/54 | 6/67 | Darlington | York | | 77014 | 7/54 | 7/67 | Darlington | Guildford | |
| 77003 | 2/54 | 12/66 | Darlington | Stourton | | 77015 | 7/54 | 7/66 | Hurlford | Hurlford | |
| 77004 | 3/54 | 12/66 | Darlington | Stourton | | 77016 | 8/54 | 3/66 | Hurlford | Hurlford | |
| 77005 | 3/54 | 11/66 | Hamilton | Motherwell | | 77017 | 8/54 | 11/66 | Hurlford | Hurlford | |
| 77006 | 3/54 | 3/66 | Hamilton | Motherwell | | 77018 | 8/54 | 11/66 | Hurlford | Hurlford | |
| 77007 | 3/54 | 11/66 | Hamilton | Hurlford | | 77019 | 9/54 | 11/66 | Hurlford | Hurlford | |
| 77008 | 4/54 | 6/66 | Perth | Motherwell | | | | | | | |
| 77009 | 6/54 | 5/66 | Perth | Motherwell | | | | | | | |
| 77010 | 6/54 | 11/65 | Darlington | Stourton | | | | | | | |
| 77011 | 6/54 | 2/66 | Darlington | Northwich | | | | | | | |

**Building details**

77000-77004 and 77010-77014 Swindon, Lot No 406
77005-77009 and 77015-77019 Swindon, Lot No 407


# Class 2 2-6-0

| BR No | Date Built | Date Withdrawn | First Shed | Final Shed | Notes | BR No | Date Built | Date Withdrawn | First Shed | Final Shed | Notes |
|---|---|---|---|---|---|---|---|---|---|---|---|
| 78000 | 12/52 | 6/65 | Oswestry | Derby | | 78046 | 10/55 | 11/66 | Hawick | St Margarets | |
| 78001 | 12/52 | 12/65 | Oswestry | Gloucester | | 78047 | 10/55 | 9/66 | Hawick | St Margarets | |
| 78002 | 12/52 | 6/66 | Oswestry | Lostock Hall | | 78048 | 10/55 | 7/64 | St Margarets | Hawick | |
| 78003 | 12/52 | 12/66 | Oswestry | Shrewsbury | | 78049 | 11/55 | 8/66 | St Margarets | St Margarets | |
| 78004 | 1/53 | 11/65 | Oswestry | Gloucester | | 78050 | 11/55 | 1/66 | Motherwell | Bathgate | |
| 78005 | 2/53 | 9/64 | Oswestry | Gloucester | | 78051 | 11/55 | 11/66 | Motherwell | Ayr | |
| 78006 | 3/53 | 12/65 | Oswestry | Gloucester | | 78052 | 11/55 | 1/66 | Motherwell | Bathgate | |
| 78007 | 3/53 | 5/67 | Oswestry | Bolton | | 78053 | 11/55 | 7/64 | Motherwell | Stirling | |
| 78008 | 3/53 | 10/66 | Oswestry | Oxley | | 78054 | 12/55 | 12/65 | Motherwell | Bathgate | |
| 78009 | 4/53 | 2/64 | Oswestry | Gloucester | | 78055 | 8/56 | 2/67 | Chester | Bolton | |
| 78010 | 12/53 | 9/66 | West Auckland | Crewe South | | 78056 | 8/56 | 7/66 | Chester | Stoke | |
| 78011 | 12/53 | 9/65 | West Auckland | Trafford Park | | 78057 | 9/56 | 5/66 | Chester | Lostock Hall | |
| 78012 | 1/54 | 5/67 | West Auckland | Bolton | | 78058 | 9/56 | 12/66 | Chester | Shrewsbury | |
| 78013 | 1/54 | 5/67 | West Auckland | Bolton | | 78059 | 9/56 | 11/66 | Chester | Crewe South | 7 |
| 78014 | 2/54 | 9/65 | West Auckland | Trafford Park | | 78060 | 10/56 | 10/66 | Aintree | Shrewsbury | |
| 78015 | 2/54 | 11/63 | West Auckland | Darlington | | 78061 | 10/56 | 11/66 | Aintree | Toton | |
| 78016 | 3/54 | 8/66 | West Auckland | Stranraer | | 78062 | 10/56 | 5/67 | Aintree | Bolton | |
| 78017 | 3/54 | 12/66 | West Auckland | Shrewsbury | | 78063 | 11/56 | 12/66 | Wigan | Shrewsbury | |
| 78018 | 3/54 | 11/66 | West Auckland | Shrewsbury | 4 | 78064 | 11/56 | 11/66 | Wigan | Toton | |
| 78019 | 3/54 | 11/66 | Kirkby Stephen | Crewe South | 5 | | | | | | |
| 78020 | 4/54 | 5/67 | Kettering | Lostock Hall | | | | | | | |
| 78021 | 5/54 | 5/67 | Kettering | Lostock Hall | | | | | | | |
| 78022 | 5/54 | 9/66 | Millhouses | Lostock Hall | 6 | | | | | | |
| 78023 | 5/54 | 5/67 | Millhouses | Bolton | | | | | | | |
| 78024 | 5/54 | 2/65 | Millhouses | Gorton | | | | | | | |
| 78025 | 6/54 | 2/65 | Grimesthorpe | Gorton | | | | | | | |
| 78026 | 6/54 | 8/66 | Canklow | Corkerhill | | | | | | | |
| 78027 | 6/54 | 9/65 | Canklow | Leicester | | | | | | | |
| 78028 | 7/54 | 2/67 | Leicester | Bolton | | | | | | | |
| 78029 | 7/54 | 10/65 | Leicester | Willesden | | | | | | | |
| 78030 | 9/54 | 10/65 | Preston | Crewe South | | | | | | | |
| 78031 | 9/54 | 10/66 | Tebay | Crewe South | | | | | | | |
| 78032 | 9/54 | 10/65 | Rhyl | Willesden | | | | | | | |
| 78033 | 9/54 | 10/65 | Rhyl | Willesden | | | | | | | |
| 78034 | 10/54 | 1/66 | Rhyl | Crewe South | | | | | | | |
| 78035 | 10/54 | 12/65 | Rhyl | Shrewsbury | | | | | | | |
| 78036 | 11/54 | 12/66 | Preston | Shrewsbury | | | | | | | |
| 78037 | 11/54 | 5/67 | Preston | Lostock Hall | | | | | | | |
| 78038 | 11/54 | 8/66 | Bescot | Shrewsbury | | | | | | | |
| 78039 | 11/54 | 9/66 | Rhyl | Shrewsbury | | | | | | | |
| 78040 | 12/54 | 1/66 | Bank Hall | Lostock Hall | | | | | | | |
| 78041 | 12/54 | 5/67 | Bank Hall | Lostock Hall | | | | | | | |
| 78042 | 12/54 | 9/65 | Bank Hall | Toton | | | | | | | |
| 78043 | 12/54 | 10/65 | Bank Hall | Willesden | | | | | | | |
| 78044 | 12/54 | 5/67 | Bank Hall | Bolton | | | | | | | |
| 78045 | 10/55 | 1/66 | Kittybrewster | Bathgate | | | | | | | |

**Building details**

78000-78009 Darlington, to WR under Swindon Lot No 402
78010-78064 Darlington

**Notes:**

1) Rescued from Woodhams, Barry scrapyard by the Standard '4' Preservation Group and preserved on the Mid-Hants Railway.
2) Rescued from Woodhams, Barry scrapyard and undergoing restoration on the Gloucestershire Warwickshire Railway, Toddington.
3) Rescued from Woodhams, Barry scrapyard and preserved on the Llangollen Railway.
4) Rescued from Woodhams, Barry scrapyard for the Market Bosworth Light Railway, and now undergoing restoration by the Darlington Railway Preservation Society
5) Rescued from Woodhams, Barry scrapyard and preserved on the Severn Valley Railway.
6) Rescued from Woodhams, Barry scrapyard by the Standard Locomotive Preservation Society and preserved on the Keighley & Worth Valley Railway.
7) Rescued from Woodhams, Barry scrapyard by the Bluebell Railway, Sheffield Park, and to be restored as a BR Standard Class 2 2-6-2T.
8) Rescued from Woodhams, Barry scrapyard and privately preserved at North Leverton

# Class 4 2-6-4T

| BR No | Date Built | Date Withdrawn | First Shed | Final Shed | Notes | BR No | Date Built | Date Withdrawn | First Shed | Final Shed | Notes |
|---|---|---|---|---|---|---|---|---|---|---|---|
| 80000 | 9/52 | 12/66 | Ayr | Corkerhill | | 80076 | 12/53 | 7/64 | Plaistow | Dumfries | |
| 80001 | 10/52 | 7/66 | Polmadie | Polmadie | | 80077 | 1/54 | 10/64 | Plaistow | Corkerhill | |
| 80002 | 10/52 | 3/67 | Motherwell | Polmadie | 1 | 80078 | 2/54 | 7/65 | Plaistow | Croes Newydd | 3 |
| 80003 | 10/52 | 3/65 | Motherwell | St Margarets | | 80079 | 3/54 | 7/65 | Plaistow | Croes Newydd | 4 |
| 80004 | 11/52 | 5/67 | Kittybrewster | Corkerhill | | 80080 | 3/54 | 7/65 | Plaistow | Croes Newydd | 11 |
| 80005 | 11/52 | 8/66 | Kittybrewster | Polmadie | | 80081 | 3/54 | 6/65 | Bletchley | Bournemouth | |
| 80006 | 11/52 | 9/66 | Polmadie | St Margarets | | 80082 | 4/54 | 9/66 | Bletchley | Eastleigh | |
| 80007 | 12/52 | 7/66 | Polmadie | Polmadie | | 80083 | 5/54 | 8/66 | Bletchley | Eastleigh | |
| 80008 | 12/52 | 7/64 | Corkerhill | Corkerhill | | 80084 | 5/54 | 6/65 | Bletchley | Redhill | |
| 80009 | 12/52 | 9/64 | Corkerhill | Corkerhill | | 80085 | 5/54 | 7/67 | Bletchley | Nine Elms | |
| 80010 | 7/51 | 6/64 | Tunbridge Wells | Brighton | | 80086 | 6/54 | 5/67 | Bury | Polmadie | |
| 80011 | 7/51 | 7/67 | Tunbridge Wells | Bournemouth | | 80087 | 6/54 | 6/64 | Bury | Eastleigh | |
| 80012 | 8/51 | 3/67 | Tunbridge Wells | Nine Elms | | 80088 | 7/54 | 6/65 | Bury | Redhill | |
| 80013 | 9/51 | 6/66 | Tunbridge Wells | Bournemouth | | 80089 | 7/54 | 10/66 | Bury | Nine Elms | |
| 80014 | 9/51 | 5/65 | Tunbridge Wells | Eastleigh | | 80090 | 8/54 | 3/65 | Bury | Dundee | |
| 80015 | 9/51 | 7/67 | Tunbridge Wells | Nine Elms | | 80091 | 9/54 | 11/66 | Kentish Town | Beattock | |
| 80016 | 9/51 | 7/67 | Tunbridge Wells | Eastleigh | | 80092 | 9/54 | 9/66 | Kentish Town | Perth | |
| 80017 | 10/51 | 9/64 | Tunbridge Wells | Eastleigh | | 80093 | 10/54 | 9/66 | Bedford | Perth | |
| 80018 | 10/51 | 4/65 | Tunbridge Wells | Eastleigh | | 80094 | 10/54 | 7/66 | Kentish Town | Feltham | |
| 80019 | 10/51 | 3/67 | Tunbridge Wells | Bournemouth | | 80095 | 11/54 | 10/66 | St Albans | Nine Elms | |
| 80020 | 10/51 | 6/65 | Kittybrewster | Corkerhill | | 80096 | 11/54 | 12/66 | Plaistow | Bournemouth | |
| 80021 | 11/51 | 7/64 | Kittybrewster | Corkerhill | | 80097 | 12/54 | 7/65 | Plaistow | Machynlleth | |
| 80022 | 11/51 | 6/65 | Polmadie | St Margarets | | 80098 | 12/54 | 7/65 | Plaistow | Machynlleth | |
| 80023 | 11/51 | 10/65 | Polmadie | Dumfries | | 80099 | 1/55 | 5/65 | Plaistow | Machynlleth | |
| 80024 | 12/51 | 8/66 | Corkerhill | Corkerhill | | 80100 | 1/55 | 7/65 | Plaistow | Shrewsbury | 5 |
| 80025 | 12/51 | 8/66 | Corkerhill | Corkerhill | | 80101 | 2/55 | 7/65 | Plaistow | Machynlleth | |
| 80026 | 12/51 | 9/66 | Polmadie | St Margarets | | 80102 | 3/55 | 12/65 | Plaistow | Eastleigh | |
| 80027 | 1/52 | 11/66 | Polmadie | Polmadie | | 80103 | 3/55 | 8/62 | Plaistow | Shoeburyness | 6 |
| 80028 | 1/52 | 9/66 | Kittybrewster | Perth | | 80104 | 3/55 | 7/65 | Plaistow | Machynlleth | |
| 80029 | 1/52 | 12/65 | Kittybrewster | Hurlford | | 80105 | 4/55 | 7/65 | Plaistow | Machynlleth | 7 |
| 80030 | 2/52 | 6/64 | Ayr/Corkerhill *3/52 | Corkerhill | | 80106 | 10/54 | 10/64 | Kittybrewster | Polmadie | |
| | | | | | | 80107 | 10/54 | 9/64 | Kittybrewster | Polmadie | |
| 80031 | 2/52 | 9/64 | Brighton | Redhill | | 80108 | 11/54 | 5/65 | Kittybrewster | Polmadie | |
| 80032 | 3/52 | 1/67 | Brighton | Bournemouth | | 80109 | 11/54 | 11/65 | Kittybrewster | Polmadie | |
| 80033 | 3/52 | 10/66 | Brighton | Feltham | | 80110 | 11/54 | 5/65 | Kittybrewster | Polmadie | |
| 80034 | 4/52 | 1/66 | Crewe North | Feltham | | 80111 | 11/54 | 11/66 | Polmadie | Beattock | |
| 80035 | 4/52 | 4/65 | Watford | Yeovil | | 80112 | 12/54 | 8/66 | Polmadie | Corkerhill | |
| 80036 | 5/52 | 11/64 | Watford | Exmouth Junction | | 80113 | 12/54 | 9/66 | Polmadie | St Margarets | |
| 80037 | 5/52 | 3/66 | Watford | Templecombe | | 80114 | 12/54 | 12/66 | Polmadie | St Margarets | |
| 80038 | 6/52 | 9/64 | Watford | Exmouth Junction | | 80115 | 12/54 | 10/64 | Polmadie | Polmadie | |
| 80039 | 6/52 | 1/66 | Bletchley | Templecombe | | 80116 | 5/55 | 5/67 | York | Polmadie | |
| 80040 | 6/52 | 5/64 | Bletchley | Exmouth Junction | | 80117 | 5/55 | 3/66 | Whitby | Polmadie | |
| 80041 | 7/52 | 3/66 | Bletchley | Templecombe | | 80118 | 6/55 | 11/66 | Whitby | Polmadie | |
| 80042 | 7/52 | 2/65 | Bletchley | Exmouth Junction | | 80119 | 6/55 | 5/65 | Whitby | Dumfries | |
| 80043 | 7/52 | 3/66 | Bletchley | Templecombe | | 80120 | 7/55 | 5/67 | Whitby | Polmadie | |
| 80044 | 8/52 | 11/64 | Derby | Corkerhill | | 80121 | 7/55 | 6/66 | Kittybrewster | Polmadie | |
| 80045 | 9/52 | 5/67 | Bedford | Polmadie | | 80122 | 8/55 | 12/66 | Kittybrewster | Greenock | |
| 80046 | 9/52 | 5/67 | Bedford | Corkerhill | | 80123 | 9/55 | 8/66 | Dundee Tay Bridge | Polmadie | |
| 80047 | 10/52 | 8/66 | Bedford | Corkerhill | | | | | | | |
| 80048 | 10/52 | 7/65 | Kentish Town | Shrewsbury | | 80124 | 9/55 | 12/66 | Dundee Tay Bridge | St Margarets | |
| 80049 | 10/52 | 6/64 | Newton Heath | Corkerhill | | | | | | | |
| 80050 | 11/52 | 11/64 | Newton Heath | Bangor | | 80125 | 10/55 | 10/64 | Stirling | Lostock Hall | |
| 80051 | 11/52 | 8/66 | Newton Heath | Corkerhill | | 80126 | 10/55 | 11/66 | Perth | Perth | |
| 80052 | 12/52 | 6/64 | Newton Heath | Corkerhill | | 80127 | 11/55 | 7/64 | Corkerhill | Corkerhill | |
| 80053 | 12/52 | 6/64 | Newton Heath | Corkerhill | | 80128 | 11/55 | 4/67 | Corkerhill | Corkerhill | |
| 80054 | 12/54 | 6/66 | Polmadie | Greenock | | 80129 | 12/55 | 10/64 | Polmadie | Lostock Hall | |
| 80055 | 12/54 | 9/66 | Polmadie | St Margarets | | 80130 | 12/55 | 8/66 | Polmadie | Polmadie | |
| 80056 | 12/54 | 10/64 | Polmadie | Lostock Hall | | 80131 | 3/56 | 5/65 | Plaistow | Bangor | |
| 80057 | 12/54 | 12/66 | Polmadie | Polmadie | | 80132 | 3/56 | 1/66 | Plaistow | Eastleigh | |
| 80058 | 1/55 | 7/66 | Polmadie | Polmadie | | 80133 | 3/56 | 7/67 | Plaistow | Nine Elms | |
| 80059 | 3/53 | 11/65 | Kentish Town | Bath Green Park | | 80134 | 4/56 | 7/67 | Plaistow | Bournemouth | |
| 80060 | 3/53 | 2/66 | Bedford | Polmadie | | 80135 | 4/56 | 7/65 | Plaistow | Shrewsbury | 8 |
| 80061 | 4/53 | 12/66 | Bedford | Polmadie | | 80136 | 5/56 | 7/65 | Plaistow | Shrewsbury | 9 |
| 80062 | 5/53 | 10/64 | Kentish Town | Stirling | | 80137 | 5/56 | 10/65 | Neasden | Nine Elms | |
| 80063 | 5/53 | 8/66 | Saltley | Corkerhill | | 80138 | 6/56 | 10/66 | Neasden | Bournemouth | |
| 80064 | 6/53 | 8/65 | Watford | Bristol Barrow Road | 2 | 80139 | 6/56 | 7/67 | Neasden | Eastleigh | |
| 80065 | 6/53 | 9/66 | Watford | Eastleigh | | 80140 | 7/56 | 7/67 | Neasden | Nine Elms | |
| 80066 | 7/53 | 6/65 | Watford | Eastleigh | | 80141 | 7/56 | 1/66 | Neasden | Nine Elms | |
| 80067 | 8/53 | 6/65 | Watford | Bristol Barrow Road | | 80142 | 8/56 | 3/66 | Neasden | Eastleigh | |
| 80068 | 8/53 | 10/66 | Watford | Feltham | | 80143 | 9/56 | 7/67 | Neasden | Nine Elms | |
| 80069 | 9/53 | 1/66 | Plaistow | Nine Elms | | 80144 | 9/56 | 5/66 | Neasden | Nine Elms | |
| 80070 | 10/53 | 6/65 | Plaistow | Eastleigh | | 80145 | 10/56 | 6/67 | Brighton | Nine Elms | |
| 80071 | 10/53 | 7/64 | Plaistow | Carstairs | | 80146 | 10/56 | 7/67 | Brighton | Bournemouth | |
| 80072 | 11/53 | 7/65 | Plaistow | Shrewsbury | | 80147 | 11/56 | 6/65 | Brighton | Bournemouth | |
| 80073 | 11/53 | 7/64 | Plaistow | Carstairs | | 80148 | 11/56 | 6/64 | Brighton | Feltham | |
| 80074 | 11/53 | 7/64 | Plaistow | Carstairs | | 80149 | 12/56 | 3/65 | Brighton | Redhill | |
| 80075 | 12/53 | 7/64 | Plaistow | Carstairs | | 80150 | 12/56 | 10/65 | Brighton | Eastleigh | |

| BR No | Date Built | Date Withdrawn | First Shed | Final Shed | Notes |
|---|---|---|---|---|---|
| 80151 | 1/57 | 5/67 | Brighton | Eastleigh | 10 |
| 80152 | 2/57 | 7/67 | Brighton | Nine Elms | |
| 80153 | 2/57 | 3/65 | Brighton | Redhill | |
| 80154 | 3/57 | 4/67 | Brighton | Nine Elms | |

## Class 3 2-6-2T

| BR No | Date Built | Date Withdrawn | First Shed | Final Shed |
|---|---|---|---|---|
| 82000 | 4/52 | 12/66 | Tyseley | Patricroft |
| 82001 | 4/52 | 12/65 | Tyseley | Bath Green Park |
| 82002 | 4/52 | 2/64 | Tyseley | Exmouth Junction |
| 82003 | 5/52 | 12/66 | Tyseley | Patricroft |
| 82004 | 5/52 | 10/65 | Tyseley | Bath Green Park |
| 82005 | 5/52 | 9/65 | Tyseley | Nine Elms |
| 82006 | 5/52 | 9/66 | Tyseley | Nine Elms |
| 82007 | 5/52 | 6/64 | Tyseley | Bristol Barrow Road |
| 82008 | 6/52 | 2/64 | Tyseley | Taunton |
| 82009 | 6/52 | 11/66 | Tyseley | Patricroft |
| 82010 | 6/52 | 4/65 | Exmouth Junction | Nine Elms |
| 82011 | 7/52 | 8/64 | Exmouth Junction | Nine Elms |
| 82012 | 7/52 | 5/64 | Exmouth Junction | Nine Elms |
| 82013 | 7/52 | 6/64 | Exmouth Junction | Nine Elms |
| 82014 | 8/52 | 5/64 | Eastleigh | Nine Elms |
| 82015 | 8/52 | 12/64 | Eastleigh | Nine Elms |
| 82016 | 8/52 | 4/65 | Eastleigh | Nine Elms |
| 82017 | 8/52 | 4/65 | Exmouth Junction | Nine Elms |
| 82018 | 9/52 | 4/66 | Redhill | Nine Elms |
| 82019 | 9/52 | 7/67 | Redhill | Nine Elms |
| 82020 | 9/54 | 9/65 | Exmouth Junction | Nine Elms |
| 82021 | 10/54 | 10/65 | Exmouth Junction | Nine Elms |
| 82022 | 10/54 | 10/65 | Exmouth Junction | Nine Elms |
| 82023 | 10/54 | 10/66 | Exmouth Junction | Nine Elms |
| 82024 | 10/54 | 1/66 | Exmouth Junction | Nine Elms |
| 82025 | 11/54 | 8/64 | Exmouth Junction | Nine Elms |
| 82026 | 11/54 | 6/66 | Kirkby Stephen | Nine Elms |
| 82027 | 11/54 | 1/66 | Kirkby Stephen | Nine Elms |
| 82028 | 12/54 | 9/66 | Darlington | Nine Elms |
| 82029 | 12/54 | 7/67 | Darlington | Nine Elms |
| 82030 | 12/54 | 12/65 | Barry | Bath Green Park |
| 82031 | 12/54 | 12/66 | Barry | Patricroft |
| 82032 | 1/55 | 5/65 | Barry | Bangor |
| 82033 | 1/55 | 9/65 | Newton Abbot | Nine Elms |
| 82034 | 1/55 | 12/66 | Newton Abbot | Patricroft |

| BR No | Date Built | Date Withdrawn | First Shed | Final Shed | Notes |
|---|---|---|---|---|---|
| 82035 | 3/55 | 8/65 | Barry | Yeovil | |
| 82036 | 4/55 | 7/65 | Barry | Bristol Barrow Road | |
| 82037 | 4/55 | 8/65 | Swansea Victoria | Bristol Barrow Road | |
| 82038 | 5/55 | 8/65 | Newton Abbot | Bristol Barrow Road | |
| 82039 | 5/55 | 7/65 | Barry | Gloucester | |
| 82040 | 5/55 | 7/65 | Barry | Gloucester | |
| 82041 | 6/55 | 12/65 | Barry | Bath Green Park | |
| 82042 | 6/55 | 8/65 | Barry | Gloucester | |
| 82043 | 6/55 | 2/64 | Barry | Bristol Barrow Road | |
| 82044 | 8/55 | 12/65 | Barry | Bath Green Park | |

## Class 2 2-6-2T

| BR No | Date Built | Date Withdrawn | First Shed | Final Shed |
|---|---|---|---|---|
| 84000 | 7/53 | 10/65 | Crewe North | Croes Newydd |
| 84001 | 7/53 | 10/64 | Crewe North | Llandudno Junction |
| 84002 | 8/53 | 4/65 | Plodder Lane | Bletchley |
| 84003 | 8/53 | 10/65 | Plodder Lane | Llandudno Junction |
| 84004 | 8/53 | 10/65 | Plodder Lane | Croes Newydd |
| 84005 | 8/53 | 10/65 | Bedford | Wellingborough |
| 84006 | 8/53 | 10/65 | Burton | Wellingborough |
| 84007 | 9/53 | 1/64 | Burton | Wellingborough |
| 84008 | 9/53 | 10/65 | Burton | Leicester |
| 84009 | 9/53 | 11/65 | Royston | Llandudno Junction |
| 84010 | 9/53 | 12/65 | Low Moor | Fleetwood |
| 84011 | 9/53 | 4/65 | Low Moor | Fleetwood |
| 84012 | 9/53 | 10/63 | Low Moor | Southport |
| 84013 | 9/53 | 12/65 | Low Moor | Stockport Edgeley |
| 84014 | 9/53 | 12/65 | Low Moor | Stockport Edgeley |
| 84015 | 10/53 | 12/65 | Low Moor | Skipton |
| 84016 | 10/53 | 12/65 | Bury | Fleetwood |
| 84017 | 10/53 | 12/65 | Bury | Stockport Edgeley |
| 84018 | 10/53 | 4/65 | Bury | Fleetwood |
| 84019 | 10/53 | 12/65 | Bury | Bolton |
| 84020 | 3/57 | 10/64 | Ashford | Llandudno Junction |
| 84021 | 3/57 | 9/64 | Ashford | Crewe Works |
| 84022 | 3/57 | 9/64 | Ashford | Crewe Works |
| 84023 | 4/57 | 9/64 | Ashford | Crewe Works |
| 84024 | 4/57 | 9/64 | Ashford | Crewe Works |
| 84025 | 4/57 | 12/65 | Ramsgate | Bolton |
| 84026 | 4/57 | 12/65 | Ramsgate | Stockport Edgeley |
| 84027 | 5/57 | 5/64 | Ramsgate | Nottingham |
| 84028 | 5/57 | 12/65 | Ramsgate | Skipton |
| 84029 | 6/57 | 6/64 | Ramsgate | Wellingborough |

## BUILDING DETAILS

80000-80009 Derby, Order No 5124
80010-80053 Brighton, Order No BR 3621
80054-80058 Derby, Order No 6231
80059-80068 Brighton, Order No BR 5271
80069-80078 Brighton, Order No BR 5788
80079-80088 Brighton, Order No BR 6166
80089-80105 Brighton, Order No BR 6167
80106-80115 Doncaster, Engine Order No 398
80116-80124 Brighton, Order No BR 6360
80125-80134 Brighton, Order No BR 6941

80135-80154 Brighton, Order No BR 7739
82000-82009 Swindon, Lot No 392
82010-82019 Swindon, Lot No 393
82020-82029 Swindon, Lot No 398
82030-82034 Swindon, Lot No 399
82035-82044 Swindon, Lot No 410

84000-84019 Crewe, Order No E484
84020-84029 Darlington

## Notes:

1) Preserved on the Keighley & Worth Valley Railway.

2) Rescued from Woodhams, Barry scrapyard by the 80064 Locomotive Group and preserved on the South Devon Railway at Buckfastleigh.

3) Rescued from Woodhams, Barry scrapyard by the Southern Steam Trust and is undergoing restoration at Swanage.

4) Rescued from Woodhams, Barry scrapyard and preserved on the Severn Valley Railway, Bridgnorth.

5) Rescued from Woodhams, Barry scrapyard and awaits restoration on the Bluebell Railway, Sheffield Park.

6) First BR Standard locomotive to be withdrawn.

7) Rescued from Woodhams, Barry scrapyard and is undergoing restoration at the Scottish Railway Preservation Society's depot, Bo'ness.

8) Rescued from Woodhams, Barry scrapyard and preserved on the North Yorkshire Moors Railway.

9) Rescued from Woodhams, Barry scrapyard and undergoing restoration by the North Staffordshire Railway Society, Cheddleton.

10) Rescued from Woodhams, Barry scrapyard by the Anglian Locomotive Group and is awaiting restoration at the Stour Valley Railway Preservation Society Centre, Chappel & Wakes Colne.

11) Rescued from Woodhams, Barry scrapyard and preserved at the Midland Railway Centre, Butterley.

12) Rescued from Woodhams, Barry scrapyard and undergoing restoration at the Midland Railway Centre, Butterley

## BR STANDARD TENDERS

| Type | Capacity Gallons Water | Tons Coal | Weight in full working order Tons Cwt | | Locomotives to which originally allocated |
|---|---|---|---|---|---|
| BR1 | 4,250 | 7 | 49 | 3 | 70000-24/30-44 72000-9, 73000-49 |
| BR1A | 5,000 | 7 | 52 | 10 | 70025-29 |
| BR1B | 4,725 | 7 | 50 | 5 | 73080-89/100-109/120-134/145-171, 75065-79, 76053-69, 92020-29/60-66/97-99 |
| BR1C | 4,725 | 9 | 53 | 5 | 73065-79/90-99/135-144 92015-19/45-59/77-86/100-139/150-164 |
| BR1D | 4,725 | 9 | 54 | 10 | 70045-54 |
| BR1E | 4,725 | 10 | 55 | 10 | 71000 |
| BR1F | 5,625 | 7 | 55 | 5 | 73110-119, 92010-14/30-44/67-76/87-96/140-149/168-202 |
| BR1G | 5,000 | 7 | 52 | 10 | 73050-52, 92000-9/203-250 |
| BR1H | 4,250 | 7 | 49 | 3 | 73053-64 |
| BR1K | 4,325 | 9 | 52 | 7 | 92165-167 |
| BR2 | 3,500 | 6 | 42 | 3 | 75000-49, 76000-44 |
| BR2A | 3,500 | 6 | 42 | 3 | 75050-64, 76045-52/70-114 77000-19 |
| BR3 | 3,000 | 4 | 36 | 17 | 78000-64 |

# Class 9F 2-10-0

| BR No | Date Built | With-drawn | First Shed | Final Shed | Notes | BR No | Date Built | With-drawn | First Shed | Final Shed | Notes |
|---|---|---|---|---|---|---|---|---|---|---|---|
| 92000 | 1/54 | 7/65 | Newport Ebbw Jct | Gloucester | 1 | 92072 | 2/56 | 1/66 | Doncaster | Kirkby-in-Ashfield | |
| 92001 | 1/54 | 1/67 | Newport Ebbw Jct | Wakefield | 1 | 92073 | 2/56 | 11/67 | Doncaster | Birkenhead | |
| 92002 | 1/54 | 11/67 | Newport Ebbw Jct | Birkenhead | | 92074 | 2/56 | 4/67 | Doncaster | Carlisle Kingmoor | |
| 92003 | 1/54 | 3/65 | Newport Ebbw Jct | Cardiff East Dock | | 92075 | 3/56 | 9/66 | Doncaster | Carlisle Kingmoor | |
| 92004 | 1/54 | 3/68 | Newport Ebbw Jct | Carnforth | | 92076 | 3/56 | 2/67 | Doncaster | Carlisle Kingmoor | |
| 92005 | 2/54 | 8/65 | Newport Ebbw Jct | York | | 92077 | 3/56 | 6/68 | Toton | Carnforth | |
| 92006 | 2/54 | 4/67 | Newport Ebbw Jct | Wakefield | 1 | 92078 | 3/56 | 5/67 | Toton | Warrington | |
| 92007 | 2/54 | 12/65 | Newport Ebbw Jct | Gloucester | | 92079 | 4/56 | 11/67 | Toton | Birkenhead | 1 |
| 92008 | 3/54 | 10/67 | Wellingborough | Warrington | | 92080 | 4/56 | 5/67 | Toton | Carlisle Kingmoor | |
| 92009 | 3/54 | 3/68 | Wellingborough | Carnforth | | 92081 | 5/56 | 2/66 | Toton | Newton Heath | |
| 92010 | 5/54 | 4/66 | March | Carlisle Kingmoor | | 92082 | 5/56 | 11/67 | Wellingborough | Birkenhead | |
| 92011 | 5/54 | 11/67 | March | Birkenhead | | 92083 | 5/56 | 2/67 | Wellingborough | Birkenhead | |
| 92012 | 5/54 | 10/67 | March | Carlisle Kingmoor | | 92084 | 5/56 | 11/67 | Wellingborough | Birkenhead | |
| 92013 | 5/54 | 9/66 | March | Saltley | | 92085 | 6/56 | 12/66 | Wellingborough | Birkenhead | |
| 92014 | 5/54 | 10/67 | March | Birkenhead | | 92086 | 6/56 | 11/67 | Wellingborough | Birkenhead | |
| 92015 | 9/54 | 4/67 | Wellingborough | Carlisle Kingmoor | | 92087 | 8/56 | 2/67 | Doncaster | Carnforth | |
| 92016 | 10/54 | 10/67 | Wellingborough | Carnforth | | 92088 | 10/56 | 4/68 | Doncaster | Carnforth | |
| 92017 | 10/54 | 12/67 | Wellingborough | Carlisle Kingmoor | | 92089 | 9/56 | 2/67 | Doncaster | Birkenhead | |
| 92018 | 10/54 | 4/67 | Wellingborough | Carlisle Kingmoor | | 92090 | 11/56 | 5/67 | Doncaster | Birkenhead | |
| 92019 | 10/54 | 6/67 | Wellingborough | Carlisle Kingmoor | | 92091 | 11/56 | 5/68 | Doncaster | Carnforth | |
| 92020 | 5/55 | 10/67 | Wellingborough | Birkenhead | 2 | 92092 | 12/56 | 10/66 | Doncaster | Birkenhead | |
| 92021 | 5/55 | 11/67 | Wellingborough | Birkenhead | 2 | 92093 | 1/57 | 9/67 | Doncaster | Carlisle Kingmoor | |
| 92022 | 5/55 | 11/67 | Wellingborough | Birkenhead | 2 | 92094 | 2/57 | 5/68 | Doncaster | Speke Jct | |
| 92023 | 5/55 | 11/67 | Wellingborough | Birkenhead | 2 | 92095 | 3/57 | 9/66 | Annesley | Warrington | |
| 92024 | 6/55 | 11/67 | Wellingborough | Birkenhead | 2 | 92096 | 4/57 | 2/67 | Annesley | Carlisle Kingmoor | |
| 92025 | 6/55 | 11/67 | Wellingborough | Birkenhead | 2 | 92097 | 6/56 | 10/66 | Tyne Dock | Tyne Dock | 3 |
| 92026 | 6/55 | 11/67 | Wellingborough | Birkenhead | 2 | 92098 | 7/56 | 7/66 | Tyne Dock | Tyne Dock | 3 |
| 92027 | 7/55 | 8/67 | Wellingborough | Speke Jct | 2 | 92099 | 7/56 | 9/66 | Tyne Dock | Tyne Dock | 3 |
| 92028 | 7/55 | 10/66 | Wellingborough | Saltley | 2 | 92100 | 8/56 | 5/67 | Toton | Birkenhead | |
| 92029 | 7/55 | 11/67 | Wellingborough | Birkenhead | 2 | 92101 | 8/56 | 10/67 | Toton | Birkenhead | |
| 92030 | 11/54 | 2/67 | New England | Wakefield | | 92102 | 8/56 | 11/67 | Toton | Birkenhead | |
| 92031 | 11/54 | 1/67 | March | Newton Heath | | 92103 | 8/56 | 5/67 | Toton | Birkenhead | |
| 92032 | 11/54 | 4/67 | March | Birkenhead | | 92104 | 8/56 | 2/67 | Toton | Birkenhead | |
| 92033 | 11/54 | 9/65 | March | Northampton | | 92105 | 9/56 | 1/67 | Wellingborough | Birkenhead | |
| 92034 | 12/54 | 5/64 | New England | Immingham | | 92106 | 9/56 | 7/67 | Wellingborough | Birkenhead | |
| 92035 | 12/54 | 2/66 | New England | Immingham | | 92107 | 9/56 | 2/67 | Wellingborough | Birkenhead | |
| 92036 | 12/54 | 12/64 | New England | New England | | 92108 | 10/56 | 11/67 | Wellingborough | Birkenhead | |
| 92037 | 12/54 | 2/65 | New England | Immingham | | 92109 | 10/56 | 11/67 | Toton | Birkenhead | |
| 92038 | 12/54 | 4/65 | New England | Langwith | | 92110 | 10/56 | 12/67 | Toton | Carlisle Kingmoor | |
| 92039 | 12/54 | 10/65 | New England | Langwith | | 92111 | 11/56 | 10/67 | Cricklewood | Birkenhead | |
| 92040 | 12/54 | 8/65 | New England | Langwith | | 92112 | 11/56 | 11/67 | Cricklewood | Birkenhead | |
| 92041 | 12/54 | 8/65 | New England | Langwith | | 92113 | 11/56 | 10/67 | Westhouses | Birkenhead | |
| 92042 | 1/55 | 12/65 | New England | Colwick | | 92114 | 11/56 | 7/67 | Westhouses | Carlisle Kingmoor | |
| 92043 | 1/55 | 7/66 | March | Carlisle Kingmoor | | 92115 | 12/56 | 2/66 | Westhouses | Speke Jct | |
| 92044 | 1/55 | 4/65 | March | Langwith | | 92116 | 12/56 | 11/66 | Westhouses | Warrington | |
| 92045 | 2/55 | 9/67 | Wellingborough | Birkenhead | | 92117 | 12/56 | 12/67 | Westhouses | Speke Jct | |
| 92046 | 2/55 | 10/67 | Wellingborough | Birkenhead | | 92118 | 12/56 | 5/68 | Westhouses | Carnforth | |
| 92047 | 2/55 | 11/67 | Wellingborough | Birkenhead | | 92119 | 1/57 | 9/67 | Westhouses | Carlisle Kingmoor | |
| 92048 | 2/55 | 9/67 | Wellingborough | Birkenhead | | 92120 | 2/57 | 7/67 | Westhouses | Birkenhead | |
| 92049 | 3/55 | 11/67 | Wellingborough | Birkenhead | | 92121 | 2/57 | 7/67 | Wellingborough | Birkenhead | |
| 92050 | 9/55 | 9/67 | Toton | Warrington | | 92122 | 2/57 | 11/67 | Wellingborough | Birkenhead | |
| 92051 | 9/55 | 10/67 | Toton | Carlisle Kingmoor | | 92123 | 3/57 | 10/67 | Wellingborough | Birkenhead | |
| 92052 | 9/55 | 8/67 | Toton | Carlisle Kingmoor | | 92124 | 3/57 | 12/66 | Wellingborough | Warrington | |
| 92053 | 9/55 | 2/66 | Toton | Warrington | | 92125 | 3/57 | 12/67 | Wellingborough | Carlisle Kingmoor | |
| 92054 | 9/55 | 5/68 | Toton | Speke Jct | | 92126 | 3/57 | 8/67 | Wellingborough | Warrington | |
| 92055 | 9/55 | 12/67 | Toton | Speke Jct | | 92127 | 4/57 | 8/67 | Wellingborough | Birkenhead | |
| 92056 | 10/55 | 11/67 | Toton | Carlisle Kingmoor | | 92128 | 4/57 | 11/67 | Toton | Carnforth | |
| 92057 | 10/55 | 10/65 | Toton | Birkenhead | | 92129 | 4/57 | 6/67 | Saltley | Carlisle Kingmoor | |
| 92058 | 10/55 | 11/67 | Toton | Carlisle Kingmoor | | 92130 | 4/57 | 5/66 | Saltley | Carlisle Kingmoor | |
| 92059 | 10/55 | 9/66 | Toton | Birkenhead | | 92131 | 5/57 | 9/67 | Saltley | Birkenhead | |
| 92060 | 11/55 | 10/66 | Tyne Dock | Tyne Dock | 3 | 92132 | 5/57 | 10/67 | Saltley | Carlisle Kingmoor | |
| 92061 | 11/55 | 9/66 | Tyne Dock | Tyne Dock | 3 | 92133 | 6/57 | 7/67 | Saltley | Birkenhead | |
| 92062 | 11/55 | 6/66 | Tyne Dock | Tyne Dock | 3 | 92134 | 6/57 | 12/66 | Saltley | Birkenhead | 9 |
| 92063 | 11/55 | 11/66 | Tyne Dock | Tyne Dock | 3 | 92135 | 6/57 | 6/67 | Saltley | Wakefield | |
| 92064 | 12/55 | 11/66 | Tyne Dock | Tyne Dock | 3 | 92136 | 7/57 | 10/66 | Saltley | Saltley | |
| 92065 | 12/55 | 4/67 | Tyne Dock | Wakefield | 3 | 92137 | 7/57 | 9/67 | Saltley | Carlisle Kingmoor | |
| 92066 | 12/55 | 5/65 | Tyne Dock | Tyne Dock | 3 | 92138 | 7/57 | 7/67 | Saltley | Speke Jct | |
| 92067 | 12/55 | 11/66 | Doncaster | Banbury | | 92139 | 7/57 | 9/67 | Saltley | Carlisle Kingmoor | |
| 92068 | 12/55 | 1/66 | Doncaster | Derby | | 92140 | 7/57 | 4/65 | New England | Langwith | |
| 92069 | 12/55 | 5/68 | Doncaster | Speke Jct | | 92141 | 12/57 | 12/65 | New England | Colwick | |
| 92070 | 1/56 | 11/67 | Doncaster | Birkenhead | | 92142 | 7/57 | 2/65 | New England | New England | |
| 92071 | 1/56 | 11/67 | Doncaster | Carlisle Kingmoor | | 92143 | 8/57 | 2/65 | New England | New England | |

# Cambridge IGCSE™

# French

Karine Harrington
Series editor: Tim Guilford

## READING AND LISTENING SKILLS

WORKBOOK

**HODDER**
EDUCATION

All images © stock.adobe.com

Every effort has been made to trace all copyright holders, but if any have been inadvertently overlooked, the Publishers will be pleased to make the necessary arrangements at the first opportunity.

Although every effort has been made to ensure that website addresses are correct at time of going to press, Hodder Education cannot be held responsible for the content of any website mentioned in this book. It is sometimes possible to find a relocated web page by typing in the address of the home page for a website in the URL window of your browser.

Hachette UK's policy is to use papers that are natural, renewable and recyclable products and made from wood grown in well-managed forests and other controlled sources. The logging and manufacturing processes are expected to conform to the environmental regulations of the country of origin.

Orders: please contact Hachette UK Distribution, Hely Hutchinson Centre, Milton Road, Didcot, Oxfordshire, OX11 7HH. Telephone: +44 (0)1235 827827. Email education@hachette.co.uk Lines are open from 9 a.m. to 5 p.m., Monday to Friday. You can also order through our website: www.hoddereducation.co.uk

ISBN: 978 1 3983 2941 6

© Karine Harrington 2022

First published in 2022 by

Hodder Education,
An Hachette UK Company
Carmelite House
50 Victoria Embankment
London EC4Y 0DZ

www.hoddereducation.co.uk

Impression number   10 9 8 7 6 5 4 3 2 1

Year        2026 2025 2024 2023 2022

Cover photo © Roman Gorielov / stock.adobe.com

Typeset in India

Printed by Hobbs the Printers Ltd, Totton, Hampshire SO40 3WX

A catalogue record for this title is available from the British Library.

# Introduction

Welcome to the *Cambridge IGCSE™ French Reading and Listening Skills Workbook*. The aim of this workbook is to provide you with further opportunity to practise the reading and listening skills you have acquired through using the IGCSE French textbook. It is designed to complement the third edition of the textbook (ISBN 978-1-5104-4755-4) and to provide additional reading and listening extracts, with accompanying exercises to help you consolidate your learning. It supports the Cambridge IGCSE French syllabus.

The sections in this workbook follow the order of your textbook. On most pages there are spaces for you to write your answers, apart from some of the longer activities which are best done on a separate piece of paper. There is no set approach to using this workbook. You may wish to use it when studying the different units to extend your learning or at a later point in the course to help with revision. The workbook is intended to be sufficiently flexible to suit whatever you feel is the best approach for your needs.

## Audio files and answers

Audio files and answers to the exercises in this workbook can be found online here:

**www.hoddereducation.co.uk/igcse_mfl_workbook_answers**

# CONTENTS

| | | Section 1: Intermediate level *Décollage* | Section 2: Higher level *En vol* |
|---|---|---|---|

## Section 1: Intermediate level

# 1 I introduce myself

## 1.1 My home

| Learning objective | Being able to identify and use noun synonyms |
|---|---|
| Grammar | Present tense |

Getting an answer right can depend on making connections between nouns that have similar meanings. This happens a lot in multiple-choice questions. For example, *dehors* and *en plein air* have connected meanings, so learn to make these connections whenever you can.

## Where do I start?

Faites correspondre le vocabulaire de la liste A au vocabulaire de la liste B.

| Liste A | | Liste B | |
|---|---|---|---|
| A | ~~la lumière~~ | 1 | le canapé |
| B | les toilettes | 2 | la couette |
| C | le sofa | 3 | le type |
| D | le tapis | 4 | le siège |
| E | la couverture | 5 | le foyer |
| F | le genre | 6 | le radiateur |
| G | le fauteuil | 7 | ~~la lampe~~ |
| H | la peinture | 8 | les WC |
| I | la maison | 9 | la moquette |
| J | le chauffage | 10 | le tableau |

| A | 7 | F | |
|---|---|---|---|
| B | | G | |
| C | | H | |
| D | | I | |
| E | | J | |

## ◆ Reading task

Lisez le texte et complétez l'activité.

Je m'appelle Alice et j'habite dans un appartement qui est assez grand, dans le centre de Toulouse. <u>Dans notre logement</u>, il y a huit pièces : le salon, la cuisine, quatre chambres et deux salles de bains. Je vais décrire chaque pièce.

Le salon est grand et les murs sont gris. Il y a deux canapés, une table basse et une grande table avec huit chaises. Nous y mangeons le dimanche ou si nous invitons mes grands-parents.

La cuisine est plus petite que le salon. Dans la cuisine, il y a des placards blancs, un grand réfrigérateur et toutes sortes d'appareils électriques comme une machine à laver, un lave-vaisselle,